KAWAII CAFÉ RAMEN

KAWAII CAFÉ RAMEN

CLASSIC, FUN, AND DELICIOUS RAMEN MEALS TO MAKE AT HOME

AMY KIMOTO-KAHN

ROCK
POINT

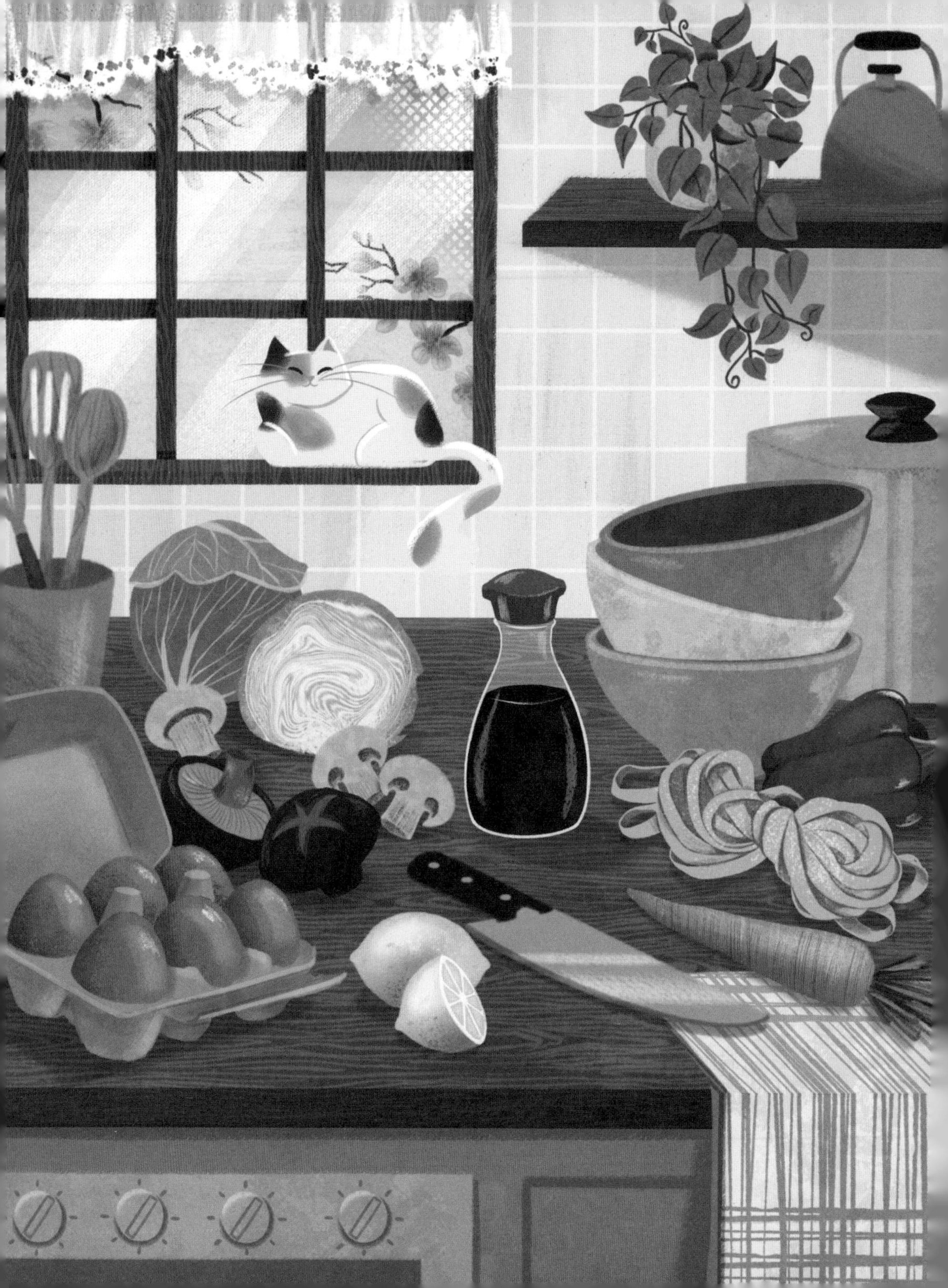

⇒ INTRODUCTION ⇐

I am a *yonsei*—a fourth-generation Japanese American. Simply put, my great-grandparents on both sides were born in Japan and were the first in my family to move to America. My parents and grandparents were both interned to concentration camps during World War II. My Great Uncle Joe Fujimoto, on my mom's side, fought in the 442nd—the only fighting unit in the U.S. Army composed entirely of those with Japanese ancestry, while their families were subject to internment. Crazy stuff.

I grew up in Fullerton, California, with an older brother and sister in the heart of Orange County. Even though I went to Japanese school on Saturdays for over eight years and studied Japanese in college, I don't speak the language much, but that's pretty common among yonsei.

I find it ironic that my parents were taken from their homes and put into camps because of their ethnicity when their generation was taught to be as American as they could be to fit in—neither of my parents has any audible accent. They understood Japanese better than they could speak it, so the language wasn't often spoken in our home. I had never even been to Japan before I wrote this book.

For most of my childhood, we ate spaghetti and meatballs more often than we ate Japanese food, but we always had Japanese rice in a cooker that kept it warm for days. I know all the yonsei out there can relate. To this day, pork chops with white fluffy rice is a favorite dish of mine. It's this melding of Japan and America that has shaped my perspective on ramen. I felt that if I didn't go to Japan and eat and see where ramen came from, and if I didn't try to learn how to make it from an expert ramen master, I wouldn't feel like I had enough knowledge to write this book.

Going to Tokyo and eating some of the best ramen and attending ramen school in Osaka was life-changing—not only for this cookbook but for me as a Japanese American, and the ramen experiences helped me develop my basic recipes and tailor them so that they are better suited for home cooks.

Closer to home, my research began at the best ramen shops near where I live in Northern California. I learned the difference between a good bowl of ramen and a great one. Most important to me are first the texture of the noodles and then the umami factor of the soup. Since high-quality ingredients were a given, I sourced mine from farmers' markets, local grocers, and Asian and Japanese markets—looking for organic where possible. I also got creative with leftovers and ingredients from my pantry.

For reference, I turned to the church cookbooks my family collected over the years from both my father's Buddhist roots and my mother's Presbyterian side. I gathered ideas from favorite recipes that have been passed down over generations and from old, treasured Japanese cookbooks that my Auntie Alice gave me. The way that I make ramen is not 100 percent traditional, but with a big family to feed, I've needed to adopt a more practical approach for making delicious meals with ingredients that are accessible to me.

In this book, you'll learn the basics of making the traditional ramen soup bases and well-known toppings, as well as my original-style versions. If you like your ramen spicy, prefer vegetarian options, or other variations, you'll find plenty of those recipes here along with special dishes, such as Chilled Cucumber Tsukemen (page 95), where noodles are served separately to be dipped into a refreshing cold broth, and a Spicy Pork Tantanmen (page 90) with a *mazamen*, or no-broth, version of Chinese Dan Dan noodles, made with a sauce of blended chili oil, chili pepper, and sesame pastes with Szechuan-numbing spices inspired by the best tantanmen I had in Tokyo.

I suggest you approach ramen as a step-by-step process that needn't be done in one day, making the soup base, noodles, and some basic toppings ahead of time. When you're ready to eat, you'll be surprised at how quickly you can pull it together.

My goal is to give you a taste of ramen culture, encourage you to learn more, and inspire you to create your own versions of ramen. All of my recipes call for one of the four basic soup bases—Tonkotsu, Shio, Miso, and Shoyu—but almost all of them can be interchanged, so don't feel like you have to use the one I've specified. Most of the ingredients for the recipes can be found in grocery stores or at farmers' markets, with only a few key ingredients, such as *dashi* (Japanese stock) and *kombu* (kelp used for flavoring soup stocks), that you may need to seek out at an Asian market or order online.

This is your chance to make your grocery shopping a cultural adventure and take your kids to a nearby Japanese grocery store. You'll be surprised by the many types of miso, *nori* (seaweed), and *shoyu* (soy sauce) there are to choose from. At our house, we've started a tradition of "build your own ramen night," with one soup base that everyone likes and a selection of DIY toppings. That's how I see ramen—it's whatever makes you happy. With *Kawaii Café Ramen*, you can enjoy ramen your way.

⇾ HOW TO BUILD A BOWL OF RAMEN ⇽

This is not a recipe but an exercise for how you would assemble a bowl of ramen after you have made one or more of the soup bases and some of the toppings. Once you are able to orchestrate the timing of your ingredients to deliver a proper bowl that has all of the elements working together, these skills can then be transferred to any bowl that you make going forward. There's an art to preparing everything in advance to ensure that all components are cooked perfectly and at the right temperatures when serving. My advice for following my recipes is to look at the prep time at the top of each recipe and the To Make in Advance section to know which components need to be made ahead of time. If you have these ready, your actual prep time to put it all together will be fairly quick.

To Make in Advance

Ramen Soup Base (page 10)

Ramen Noodles (page 24)

Ramen Toppings (page 26)

To Prep Before You Begin

Additional Toppings and Condiments*

In addition to Ramen Toppings (page 26), there are a myriad of additional toppings and condiments for topping your bowls of ramen.

Toppings: negi (green onion), sweet corn, parsley, butter, onions, yuzu citrus, bean sprouts, spinach, ginger, Japanese mushrooms (shitake, kirurage), kamaboko (Japanese fish cake), and takana (spicy pickled mustard greens)

Condiments: white pepper, shoyu (soy sauce), shichimi-togarashi (mixed chili pepper spice), chili paste, fresh garlic, vinegar, chili oil, sesame seeds, and curry powder

1 Place a pot of water to boil for your noodles. When it comes to a boil, make sure you wait until you have your soup base heated and your toppings ready to go before you cook your noodles.

2 In a large pot, bring your base or your base and stock (depending on the soup base you're using) to a boil, then lower heat and let simmer until it's ready to serve. Right before serving, crank it back up to boil.

3 (Optional) Ladle some of the boiling noodle water into your ramen bowl(s) for a couple of minutes to warm them before plating. Return the water to the pot to return to a boil.

4 Boil the noodles (if fresh, boil for about 1 minute; if packaged, boil for about 2 minutes). As soon as the noodles are done, shake out all of the excess water and lay them gently into your warmed serving bowls by folding them on top of each other so they do not look messy. Be prepared to assemble the entire bowl and serve it as soon as your noodles come out of the water!

5 Pour piping hot soup over the noodles in each bowl. Place your ramen and additional toppings on top. You did it! Now sit down, savor the moment, and enjoy slurping it all away!

RAMEN SOUP BASES & NOODLES

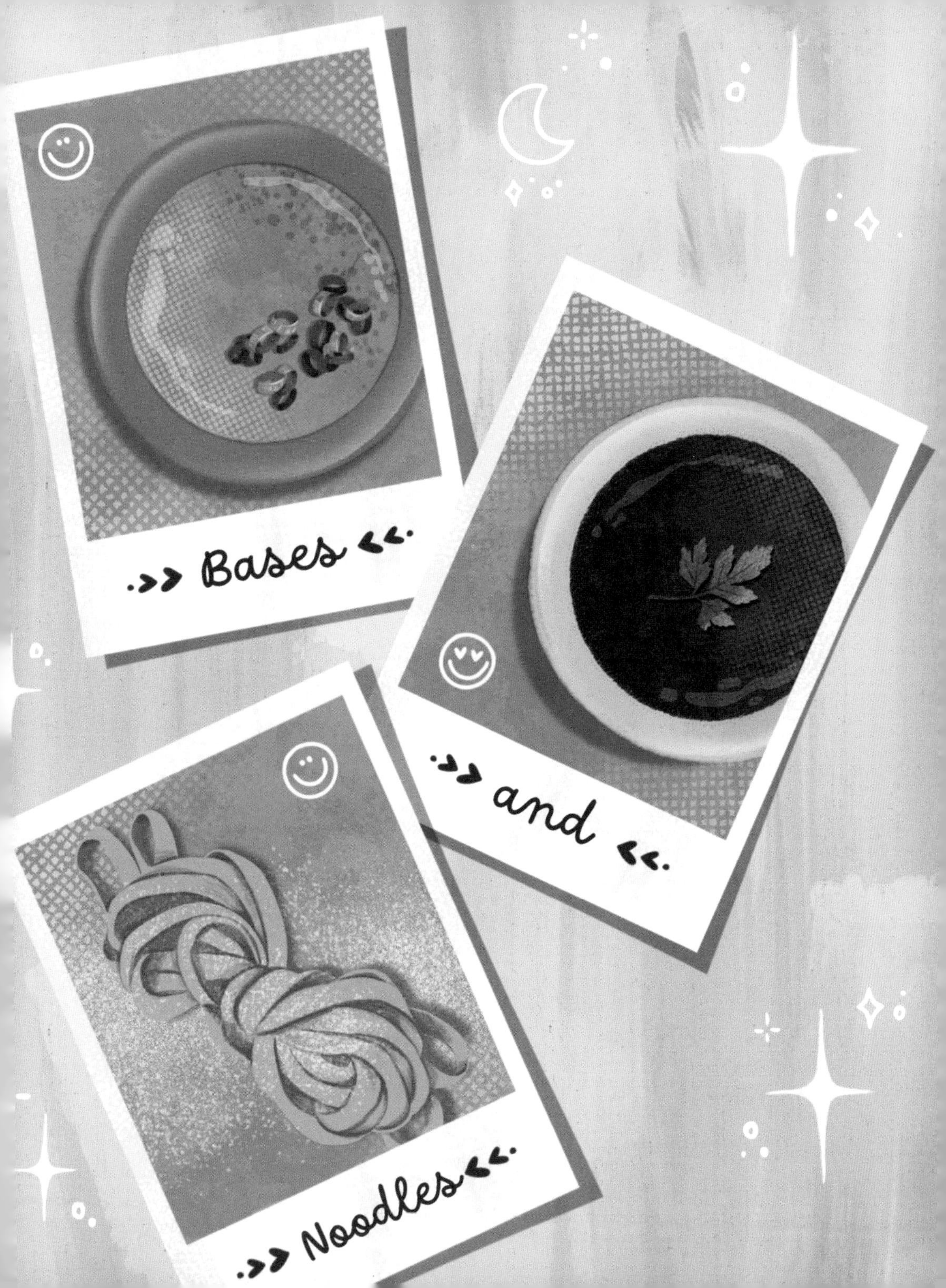
Bases
and
Noodles

⇥ MISO BASE ⇤

Level	1
Serves	12
Prep Time	45 minutes

I've made a super flavorful miso base, or *misodare*, that can be enjoyed any time. Store it in the refrigerator, and when needed, you can make individual servings or enough to feed your whole family—this base offers the convenience of a one-person portion or a meal for twelve, all according to the base-to-stock ratio (3 tablespoons Miso Base to 1 cup, or 240 ml, chicken or vegetable stock). The Miso Base can be refrigerated for up to 1 week or frozen for 1 month.

Ingredients

1 medium carrot, peeled and cut into large dice

½ onion, peeled and cut into large dice

½ apple, cored, peeled and cut into large dice

1 celery stalk, cut into large dice

3 garlic cloves

½ cup (120 ml) bacon fat (recommended), ghee, or coconut oil

2 tbsp sesame oil, divided

1½ cups (340 g) ground pork

2 tsp grated ginger

1 tsp sriracha

2 tbsp soy sauce

1 tsp kelp granules (optional but recommended)

1 tbsp apple cider vinegar

1 tsp salt

1 tbsp ground sesame seed paste or tahini

¾ cup (180 ml) Shiro miso (white miso, which is lighter and sweeter)

¾ cup (180 ml) Akamiso miso (red miso, which is darker and saltier)

Low-sodium chicken or vegetable stock (2 cups, or 480 ml, per serving based on the number of servings)

1 Add the carrot, onion, apple, celery, and garlic to a food processor. Pulse into a fine chop. It is better to use a food processor, but if you don't have one, finely chop these ingredients by hand.

2 Add the bacon fat and 1 tablespoon sesame oil to a large skillet over medium-high heat. Add the finely chopped fruit and vegetables and cook until onions are translucent and apple is tender, stirring occasionally, for 10 to 12 minutes. When done, turn heat down to medium-low.

3 Add your ground pork to the cooked vegetable mixture. Cook for 8 to 10 minutes until the meat is no longer pink. Stir in the ginger, sriracha, soy sauce, kelp granules, apple cider vinegar, and salt. Incorporate well.

4 Return the entire mixture to the food processor and pulse until pork is finely ground. It is better to use a food processor, but if you don't have one, then use a potato masher or wooden spoon to break the mixture into very small pieces in the skillet.

5 Add the sesame seed paste and miso to the ground pork mixture and mix well. It should have the consistency of a thick paste. Your base is done.

6 Bring the miso base and chicken or vegetable stock to a boil (depending on the number of people you are serving, use the ratio of 3 tablespoons miso base to 1 cup (240 ml) chicken or vegetable stock). Lower heat and let simmer until it's ready to serve. Use about 2 cups (480 ml) soup per serving. Right before serving, crank the heat back up to boil the soup.

7 Pour 2 cups soup (480 ml) over each bowl of noodles. Top each bowl with desired toppings. (See How to Build a Bowl of Ramen on page 10 for help with timing the orchestration of your ramen components.)

⇢ TONKOTSU BASE ⇠

Level	3
Serves	10
Prep Time	4 hours, plus time to make Chashu
Equipment	30-quart (29 L) pressure cooker (read and follow the manufacturer's instructions; if you do not have a pressure cooker this size, prepare in 2 or 3 batches in a smaller slow cooker or electric pressure cooker, or make it in a large stockpot and cook over low heat for 15 to 20 hours, until the broth is a creamy white color and all the meat has fallen off the bones.)

The tonkotsu base is the holy grail of ramen soup bases, and this recipe follows the traditional recipe I learned to make from Sensei Miyajima Rikisai at the Miyajima Ramen School in Osaka, Japan. *Tonkotsu*, known as "white soup," comes from two different regions in Japan. This version comes from the Kanto region of Tokyo. It uses a double-soup method, where two separate broths are combined right before serving, making a more complex and flavorful soup. *Note: If the soup doesn't obtain its signature creamy white color, you can blend it after all bones are removed and it will emulsify to achieve this.*

To Make In Advance

Chashu, with its braising liquid (page 32)

Seabura (boiled pork back fat)

1½ lbs (700 g) pork back fat, cut into strips

Water, to cover

Tonkotsu Soup

½ lb (225 g) chicken feet, cleaned, extra skin removed and nails cut off (approximately 6 feet)

8 to 10 lbs (3.6 to 4.5 kg) pork knuckles/trotters, pounded with a mallet to release marrow

1 lb (455 g) potatoes, unpeeled and sliced in big chunks

5 qts (4.7 L) water

Shiodare (salt flavor component)

1 large rectangular piece kombu (about 10 inches, or 25 cm, long), cut into large squares

1 large or 2 small dried shiitake mushrooms, crumbled

1 qt (1 L) water

2 tbsp bonito flakes

1½ cups (300 g) baby clams

½ cup (140 g) table salt

Shoyudare (soy sauce flavor component)

Equal parts Shiodare and Chashu braising liquid (do not assemble until ready to use)

1 Before cooking, you must have the chashu with its braising liquid on hand to use later.

2 Make the Seabura: Place the pork back fat in a large pot, cover with water, bring to a boil, and simmer for 4 hours, uncovered.

3 Make the Tonkotsu Soup: In a separate pot of boiling water, blanch the chicken feet, drain, and then add them to the pressure cooker along with the pork knuckles or trotters and the potatoes. Cover with up to 5 quarts (4.7 L) water, making sure the total volume of water and food combined does not exceed half of the pot.

4 Leave your pressure regulator weight off of the vent pipe. Turn heat to high until steam flows from the vent pipe (this may take up to 20 minutes) and continue to let vent for 10 minutes more while the steam displaces the air in the cooker. Maintain high heat setting and start timing your cooking when the regulator weight begins to jiggle or rock. It may appear as if it is leaking, but this is normal. Regulate the heat so that the weight only jiggles 1 to 4 times per minute. Start a timer and cook for 1 hour.

5 Make the Shiodare: In a medium pot, bring the kombu, shiitake, and 4 cups (950 ml) water to a boil. Lower the heat and simmer for 5 minutes. Drain the kombu and shiitake and put the soup into a clean medium pot.

6 Return this drained soup to the stove, add the bonito flakes, and heat to a boil, then simmer for 5 minutes. Drain the bonito flakes and put soup into your other empty pot, pressing the flakes to release all their liquid.

7 Return this drained soup to the stove and add the clams, bring to a boil, then simmer for 5 minutes. Remove the clams with a sieve and measure out 1 quart or 4 cups (1 L) soup into your other empty pot (you will have a minimal amount to discard). Whisk in ½ cup (140 g) table salt. Note that the salt-to-soup ratio should be 20 percent, resulting in a very salty soup base for Shiodare.

8 After 1 hour, take the pressure cooker off the heat and allow the pressure gauge to return to 0 (zero) before gently removing the cover. Push down the pork bones to get the bone fat out and make the soup creamier and thicker. Cook on a medium-low heat with the cover off for about 1 hour longer, mixing periodically.

9 Directly into your serving bowls, add 1 tablespoon of your Chashu braising liquid and 1 tablespoon shiodare per serving to make a shoyudare.

10 Drain and remove the pork back fat that has been simmering. Cut the strips into smaller 2-inch (5 cm) pieces. Into a medium bowl, take a large-holed sieve and push a couple of pieces at a time through the sieve so that you see it come through the other side in small little bits. Repeat until all pieces are pushed through. Your Seabura is ready. Set aside.

11 Strain all of the solids from the tonkotsu soup in the pressure cooker and transfer the soup to a separate pot and keep warm. Right before serving, crank it up to a boil.

12 Remove the chashu from its braising liquid and cut into ¼-inch (6 mm) thick rounds. Sauté your sliced pork in a skillet for 1 to 2 minutes to render the fat and make the slices crispy before placing on top of ramen. Use as many slices as you'd like to serve on your ramen; typical amounts vary from 1 to 3 slices.

13 To assemble your bowl, add 1 cup (240 ml) piping hot tonkotsu soup to your shoyudare (step 9) and 1 tablespoon of the seabura (step 10) to each serving portion, then add your noodles and place the sliced chashu on top along with desired toppings. (See How to Build a Bowl of Ramen on page 10 for help with timing the orchestration of your ramen components.)

⇝ SHOYU BASE ⇜

Level	2
Serves	12
Prep Time	8 to 10 hours, plus 30 minutes to strain

If you've made my Tonkotsu Base (page 16), then you have a basic *shoyudare*, or strong soy sauce flavor base, with which you can combine with any stock or fat to make a simple shoyu ramen. This recipe combines the stock, shoyudare, and fat into one. With this recipe I've slow-cooked oxtail sections within my broth in a good crock pot, which helps render the fat from the bones without having to constantly stir. You could also make this in a slow cooker, large Dutch oven, or heavy-duty pot. The oxtail adds a meaty goodness and complexity to the fat component that complements the soy sauce. You'll have to go to an Asian market to find *dashi*, or Japanese stock, which comes in granular form—there are many varieties to choose from, so just make sure to pick one that has bonito fish as the primary ingredient. It's also important to have dried shiitake mushrooms, as they'll give a more intense flavor to the soup than fresh ones. The final soup will taste overly salty, but when the noodles are added in, they will soak up the sauce and balance it out.

Ingredients

4 tbsp bacon fat (recommended), ghee, or coconut oil

2 medium carrots, peeled, cut into large dice

½ onion, peeled and cut into large dice

3 green onions, cut into thirds

1 apple, cored and quartered (with skin on)

2 celery stalks, cut into thirds

5 garlic cloves, peeled and left whole

5 dried shiitake mushrooms*, broken up into small pieces

1 whole organic chicken

4 medium oxtail sections, roughly 2 inches (5 cm) long

1 lemon, quartered

2 qts (2.2 L) low-sodium chicken stock

¾ cup (180 ml) high-grade soy sauce

4 tsp dashi granules* (Japanese stock)

2 tbsp salt

½ tsp white pepper

1 bay leaf

*It's important to use dried shiitake mushrooms, as they'll give a more intense flavor to the soup than fresh ones.

*Dashi, or Japanese stock, comes in granular form—there are many varieties to choose from, so just make sure to pick one that has bonito fish as the primary ingredient. You'll find it at an Asian market.

1 In a crock pot, slow cooker, large Dutch oven, or heavy-duty pot, combine the bacon fat, carrots, onion, green onions, apple, celery, garlic, and dried shiitake mushrooms.

2 Add the whole chicken, oxtails, and lemon, then pour over the chicken stock, followed by the soy sauce, dashi, salt, pepper, and bay leaf; the stock should almost cover the chicken.

3 Set the crock pot or slow cooker to high and let cook for 10 hours. If using a large Dutch oven or pot, bring to a boil over a high heat and set in an oven preheated to 200ºF (90ºC) for 8 to 10 hours. When the oxtail meat easily falls off the bone, your soup is done.

4 With a slotted spoon, remove all of the larger solids and discard. Strain the remaining solids with a finer sieve into a large pot. You should have a light brown, glossy, and fat-rich soup. At this point the stock can be refrigerated for up to 2 weeks or frozen for 1 month.

5 In a separate saucepan, bring the shoyu base to a boil, then lower the heat and let simmer until it's ready to serve. Use about 2 cups (480 ml) per serving. Right before serving, crank it back up to a boil.

6 Pour 2 cups soup (480 ml) over each bowl of noodles. Top each bowl with desired toppings. (See How to Build a Bowl of Ramen on page 10 for help with timing the orchestration of your ramen components.)

SHIO BASE

Level **1**

Serves **12**

Prep Time 45 minutes

If you've made my Tonkotsu Base (page 16), then you have a basic *shiodare*, or strong salt flavor base, with which you can combine any stock or fat to make a simple shio ramen. This recipe is a variation of shiodare but adds additional flavor so that you can simply combine it with a chicken or vegetable stock for a flavorful soup. This recipe starts off with the same components as the Miso Base (page 14), but I've added fresh and dried shiitake mushrooms to give it added depth.

Ingredients

1 medium carrot, peeled and chopped

½ onion, peeled and cut into large dice

3 green onions, white part only, chopped

½ apple, peeled, cored, and chopped

1 celery stalk, cut into large dice

3 garlic cloves

5 fresh shiitake mushrooms

½ cup (120 ml) bacon fat (recommended), ghee, or coconut milk

1 tbsp sesame oil

3 tsp dashi granules (Japanese stock)

2 tbsp fleur de sel or salt of your choice

Broth

Unsalted butter (2 tbsp per serving)

Low-sodium chicken or vegetable stock (2 cups, or 480 ml, per serving)

Mirin (1 tsp per serving)

1 large rectangular piece kombu (about 10 inches, or 25 cm, long), cut into large squares

Dried shiitake mushrooms, crumbled (2 mushrooms per serving)

1 In a food processor, combine the carrot, onion, green onions, apple, celery, garlic, and fresh shiitake mushrooms and process until very finely chopped, almost like a paste. It is better to use a food processor, but if you don't have one, finely chop these ingredients by hand.

2 In a medium pot, warm the bacon fat and sesame oil over medium-high heat. Add the finely chopped vegetables and cook, stirring occasionally, until the onions are translucent and the apple is tender, 10 to 12 minutes. Add the dashi and fleur de sel and mix well.

3 To make the broth, add the butter to a large saucepan over medium-high heat. Once the butter starts to brown and smells nutty, add the stock, mirin, kombu, and mushrooms. Bring to a boil, reduce heat, and let simmer for at least 15 minutes, then remove solids with a sieve. Add the Shio Base to the broth (depending on the number of people you are serving, it's 3 tablespoons shio base to every 1 cup, or 240 ml, broth). Lower heat and let simmer until it's ready to serve. Use about 2 cups (480 ml) soup per serving. Right before serving, crank the heat back up to boil.

4 Pour 2 cups (480 ml) soup over each bowl of noodles and add your desired toppings. (See How to Build a Bowl of Ramen on page 10 for help with timing the orchestration of your ramen components.)

⇌ SPICY BASE ⇌

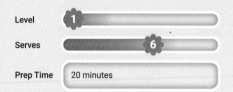

Level	1
Serves	6
Prep Time	20 minutes

I most often use this base with the Miso Base (page 14), but it can be used with any base to add a rich and spicy complexity that isn't mouth-numbing but definitely gives it a nice kick. Add more or less of it depending on how spicy you like your ramen.

Ingredients

16 small shishito peppers, whole (substitute 3 green bell peppers, seeded)

2 green chili peppers, seeded and quartered

2 tsp red pepper flakes

½ cup (120 ml) sesame oil

1 In a blender, combine the green bell peppers, green chili peppers, and red pepper flakes. Slowly add in the sesame oil to emulsify.

2 Add ½ cup (120 ml) of spicy base for each 2-cup (480 ml) serving to any ramen soup base.

⇥ COLD NOODLE BROTH ⇤

Level **1**

Serves **6**

Prep Time 30 minutes

My brother-in-law, Victor, got this recipe from his uncle who runs a small restaurant in Yokohama, Japan. The broth is very strong, so use it sparingly. It's more like a flavorful sauce than a soup, so don't overserve this one. It's super simple and perfect for a nice hot day.

Ingredients

3½ cups (360 ml) water

1½ cups (150 g) sugar (I prefer baker's sugar, as it's finer and dissolves quicker)

1½ cups (360 ml) mirin (rice wine vinegar)

½ cup (120 ml) shoyu (soy sauce)

Sesame oil

1 In a medium pot over medium-high heat, add the water, sugar, vinegar, and shoyu. Mix well until the sugar dissolves.

2 Remove from the heat and let cool before using the broth.

3 Right before serving, add a couple of drops of sesame oil to each serving. Serve over cold noodles with your toppings of choice.

⇾ RAMEN NOODLES ⇽

Level	3
Serves	8
Prep Time	3 hours

These noodles can be wrapped in individual portions and frozen for up to one month. You will need a pasta machine, and I'd recommend using an electric mixer with a dough hook. Remember, there are lots of other, easier noodle alternatives* that are perfectly fine. If you do venture down the homemade noodle path, then keep this in mind: a perfect noodle has a yellow hue, is cooked al dente, and has a chewy and elastic yet firm texture that holds up to the soup without getting soggy.

Ingredients

2 tsp "baked baking soda" (page 25) or kansui powder

1¼ cups (300 ml) water (if you are hand-kneading, change water quantity to 1½ cups, or 360 ml)

3½ cups (490 g) bread flour, plus extra for dusting

½ cup (60 g) cake flour

1 cup (150 g) wheat flour

1 tbsp salt

Cornstarch, for dusting

*Any of these store-bought alternatives will work, just throw out those salty flavor packets:

- fresh noodles from a ramen shop
- fresh packaged noodles that come with a soup-base packet
- dried ramen noodles for instant ramen
- dried chuka soba noodles (chuka soba translates to "Chinese noodle," which are, in fact, ramen noodles)
- gluten-free packaged ramen noodles or rice ramen noodles

1 In a small bowl, combine the baked baking soda or kansui powder and water until it dissolves.

2 In a stand mixer fitted with a dough hook, combine the bread, cake, and wheat flours; kansui water; and salt. Mix for 10 minutes on the lowest speed until the dough forms little pellets. If you need to, add up to 5 additional teaspoons of water. The dough is ready when it still feels dry but comes together when squeezed with your hand.

3 Tip the dough onto a floured board and knead into a ball for at least 10 minutes. Alternatively, you can put your dough in a plastic zip-top bag and form it into a ball so that it is easier to bring together and knead. When you are ready to make your pasta, set up your pasta machine so that it is stable and won't slip from your work surface.

4 Cut your dough ball into 8 equal-size pieces and use one piece at a time, keeping the rest wrapped tightly with plastic wrap or sealed in your zip-top bag and refrigerated. Roll out one piece until it resembles a flat, long shape. Sprinkle with some cornstarch so it doesn't stick to the pasta maker. Pass it through your pasta maker on the largest setting; it will be a bit rough at the edges, but don't worry about how it looks. Fold it over on itself and pass it through the machine again.

5 Reduce the machine width to 2 and pass through. Fold it over on itself and pass it through again. Reduce the machine width to 4 and pass it through only once. You will now have one long strip of dough. Cut this strip in half vertically. Reduce the machine width to 6 and pass through one of the halves twice. Repeat with the other half. Now your dough is ready to run through the noodle cutter attachment.

6 The 2 strips will yield enough noodles for 1 bowl of ramen. Repeat step 5 for the remaining dough pieces from step 4. Sprinkle each batch of noodles with additional cornstarch, lifting up the noodles to separate and lightly coat them, then pack them individually in plastic wrap. Let them sit in the refrigerator for at least a day before using. If you are planning to use them later, put them in individual zip-top bags and store them in the freezer for up to 1 month.

7 Cook the fresh pasta in a pot of boiling water. Depending on the number of portions, cook for 1 to 2 minutes. Shake out all excess water and lay a portion in your bowl of hot soup by folding them over onto each other so they do not look messy. Then add the soup and toppings.

HOW TO MAKE "BAKED" BAKING SODA

Baked baking soda replaces a Japanese ingredient known as *kansui* that is often difficult to find and that gives ramen noodles their signature yellow hue and firmness. Harold McGee, the king of kitchen science, discovered that by baking baking soda, you could get the same effect as the kansui. Spread ¼ cup (55 g) baking soda on a foil-lined baking sheet and place it in an oven preheated to 275°F (135°C) for 1 hour. As this recipe only calls for 2 teaspoons, you can save the remainder in a zip-top bag. Just fold up the baking soda in the foil to make it easier to put in a storage bag.

RAMEN TOPPINGS

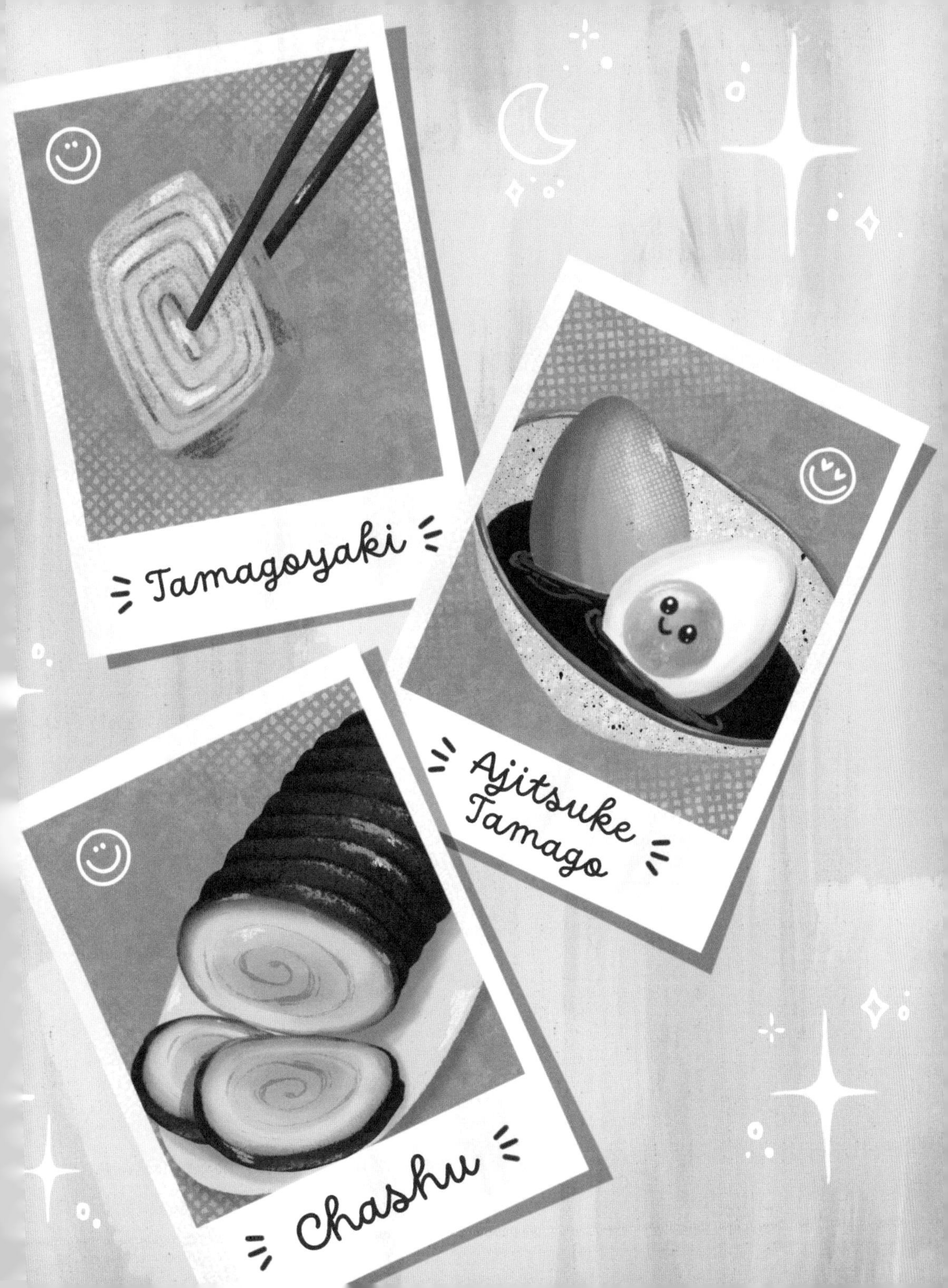
Tamagoyaki
Ajitsuke Tamago
Chashu

⇒ TAMAGOYAKI (JAPANESE OMELET) ⇐

Level **2**

Serves **4**

Prep Time 10 minutes

You will need a Japanese tamagoyaki pan (it's rectangular) to get a visually appealing omelet. If you don't have one, a regular skillet will work, but you won't end up with the uniform rectangular shape that distinguishes this omelet.

Ingredients

3 eggs

1 green onion, thinly sliced

1 tsp shoyu (soy sauce)

1 tsp sugar

¼ tsp salt

Nonstick cooking spray

1 In a medium bowl, whisk the eggs with the green onion, shoyu, sugar, and salt until foamy.

2 Over medium-high heat, warm 1 teaspoon vegetable oil in a tamagoyaki pan or skillet. Drip a tiny bit of egg in the pan; if it sizzles on contact, the pan is sufficiently hot. Add about a quarter of the egg mixture to the pan and tilt the pan so that the egg mixture covers the bottom in a thin, even layer. The egg will start cooking quickly so you'll need to move fast.

3 Using chopsticks, gently roll the egg mixture tightly toward you from the part of the pan farthest from the handle.

4 Quickly add a little more cooking spray to the exposed part of the pan.

5 Pour another quarter of the egg mixture into the pan, lifting up the cooked portion to get some egg mixture underneath it to cook.

6 Roll the egg mixture away from you this time as it combines and attaches to the cooked egg layer. Nudge it to the back to the front of the pan, where you started before.

7 Repeat two more times until you've used all the egg; the omelet will obviously increase in size with each layer.

8 Roll the omelet out of the pan and you should have a rectangular-shaped block with your layers of egg. Let cool and slice vertically before serving.

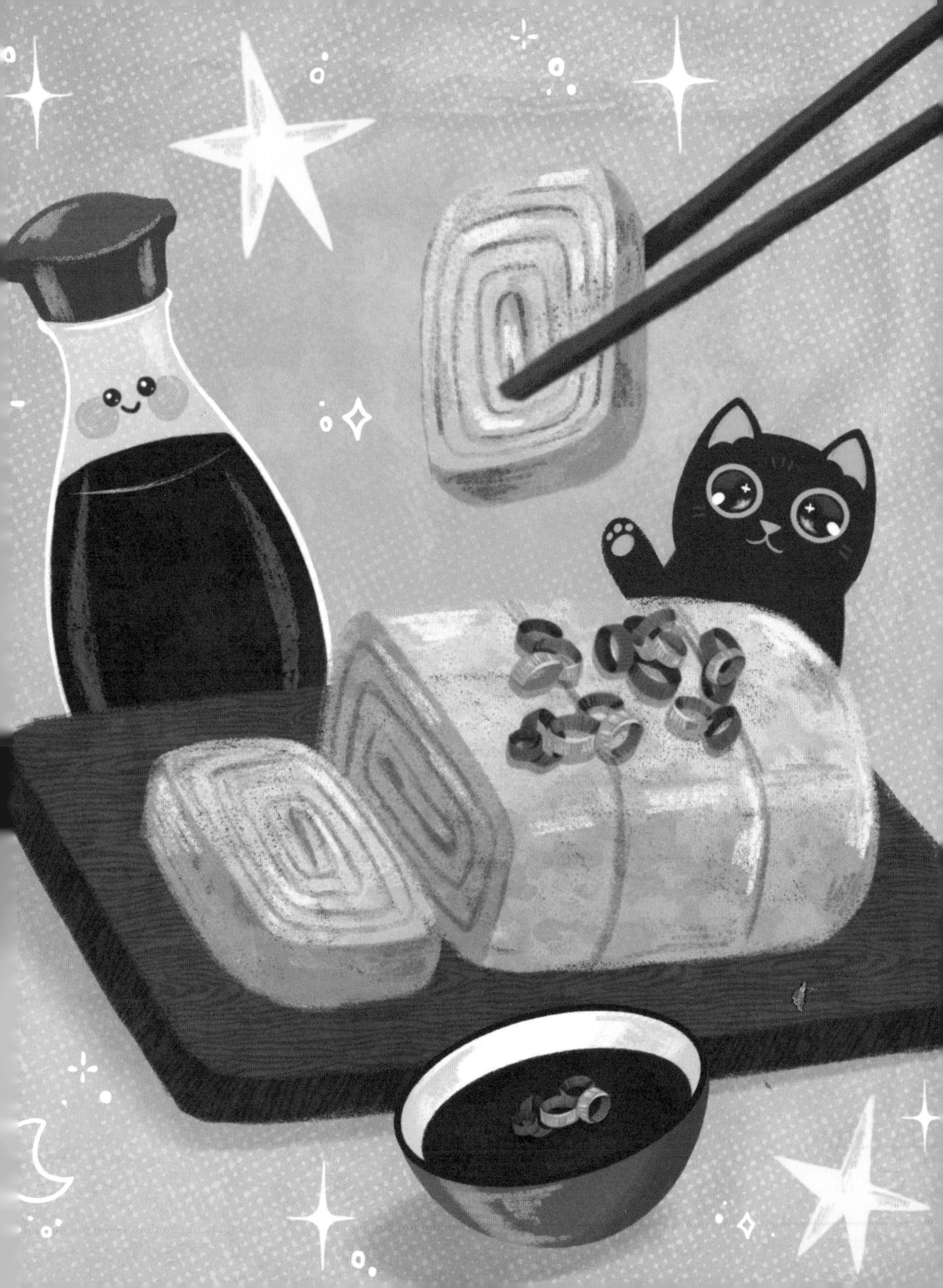

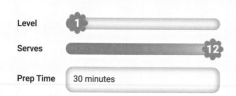

⇥ MENMA (SEASONED BAMBOO SHOOTS) ⇤

Level	1
Serves	12
Prep Time	30 minutes

This is a popular topping for ramen, and there is a world of difference between fresh bamboo shoots and canned. If you can't find fresh bamboo, I would forgo using it entirely. You can find fresh bamboo in most Asian grocery stores; you can recognize it by its signature conical shape.

Ingredients

1 lb (455 g) fresh bamboo shoots

1 tbsp sesame oil

2 cups (480 m) water

3 tsp dashi granules

1 tbsp shoyu (soy sauce)

1 tbsp sake

2 tsp sugar

1 tsp salt

1 Cut the bamboo shoots in half lengthwise and then into thin slices horizontally.

2 In a large sauté pan over medium-high heat, combine the sesame oil, water, dashi, shoyu, sake, sugar, and salt. Add the bamboo shoots.

3 Heat, uncovered, until the bamboo has absorbed most of the liquid, about 20 minutes. Remove from heat and store in an airtight container. Will keep for up to 1 week in the refrigerator or frozen for up to 1 month.

POACHED EGGS

Level 1

Makes: As many as you need

Prep Time: 10 minutes

Poached eggs aren't as labor-intensive as Marinated Half-Cooked Eggs (page 34), and their runny center provides an instant sauce to swirl into ramen soup. Cook them ahead of time, and when your other ramen components are ready to assemble, just warm the poached eggs in the ramen cooking water for 10 seconds before gently transferring to the bowls.

Ingredients

Dash of white vinegar or squeeze of lemon juice

Eggs (as many as you need)

1 Fill a medium pot with about 1½ inches (4 cm) water and bring to a boil over high heat. Add the white vinegar or lemon juice; this will help the eggs to coagulate quicker and reduce the amount of feathering around the edges, but don't add too much or the eggs will taste sour. Once the water comes to a boil, reduce to just above a simmer.

2 Crack an egg into a small ramekin or cup. If poaching more than one egg, prepare up to 3 ramekins at a time. (I don't recommend cooking more than 3 at a time.)

3 Gently slide the eggs out of the ramekins and into the simmering water. Take care not to crowd the pan.

4 Cook the eggs until the whites are opaque, about 3½ minutes.

5 With a slotted spoon, transfer the cooked eggs to a paper towel to drain. If not using immediately, store in a water bath in an airtight container and refrigerate for up to 2 days. When your other ramen components are ready to assemble, just warm the poached eggs in the ramen cooking water for 10 seconds before gently transferring to the bowls.

CHASHU (BRAISED PORK)

Level	2
Serves	6
Prep Time	4 hours cooking time

Chashu is one of the most popular ramen toppings. It can vary in flavor, size, and fat content. Its origin, just like ramen, stems from the Chinese *char-siu*, roasted or barbecued pork, but Japanese chashu is completely different. It's not red, has more fat and tenderness, and is typically braised rather than barbecued. Braising calls for cooking it in liquid at low heat until the tough collagen in the meat breaks down. The result is a melt-in-your mouth experience.

Ingredients

2 lbs (900 g) pork shoulder or other part with fat, cut into 4-to 5 inch-wide (10 to 13 cm) pieces, rolled up into a round bundle, and tightly trussed with cooking string

2½ qts or 10 cups (2.8 L) water

1 qt or 4¼ cups (1 L) dark shoyu (soy sauce)

2½ cups (500 g) sugar

¾ cup (180 ml) mirin (sweet rice wine)

1 green onion, thinly sliced

1 tbsp grated ginger

1 Combine the pork with the water, shoyu, sugar, mirin, onion, and ginger in a large pot over high heat. Bring to a boil, reduce to a simmer, and cook until the pork is tender, about 4 hours. Skim off any scum that floats to the surface.

2 Remove the pork from the liquid. Insert a medium-thick wooden skewer into the center of the meat. If it comes out clean, the pork is done.

3 When you are ready to use it, take the pork out of the liquid. Save the liquid for Marinated Half-Cooked Eggs (page 34) or adding to your Shoyu Ramen Base; do not throw this away! Let the pork rest for at least 2 hours or overnight in the braising liquid in the refrigerator to make it easier to slice (overnight is best as the pork will continue to soak up the juices in that time).

4 Sauté your sliced pork in a skillet for 1 to 2 minutes to render the fat and make the slices crispy before placing on top of ramen. Cut into ¼-inch-thick (6 mm) rounds. Use as many slices as you'd like to serve on your ramen; typical amounts vary from 1 to 3 slices.

ROASTED NORI (SEAWEED)

vel 1

akes: As many as you need (2 squares per portion)

ep Time: 2 minutes

These days you can find roasted and flavored seaweed in grocery stores, coffee shops, and even vending machines. I prefer to roast my own because some of the varieties out there are too oily or aren't crunchy enough for me.

gredients

- ieets of nori (seaweed)
- onstick cooking spray or sesame oil
- ea or kosher salt

1 Spray both sides of each nori sheet with cooking spray or wipe sesame oil over it using a folded paper towel.

2 Over a low flame on a gas stove, gently waft the seaweed back and forth on both sides until crisp.

3 Set the finished roasted seaweed sheet on a paper towel and repeat with additional sheets.

4 Sprinkle each sheet with salt and stack them about 4 or 5 high.

5 Cut each stack into quarters with a sharp chef's knife or with kitchen shears.

BENI SHOGA (PICKLED GINGER)

vel 1

erves 30

ep Time: 2 weeks

Most recipes for beni shoga call for fresh shiso, but since store-bought umeboshi vinegars tend to have shiso leaves in their liquid, I forgo using fresh shiso.

gredients

- oz (170 g) ginger root (about 3 medium stalks)
- cup (240 ml) umeboshi (pickled Japanese plum) vinegar*
- tbsp salt
- tbsp sugar
- tbsp mirin (sweet rice wine)
- tsp yellow mustard seeds

You can purchase umeboshi vinegar at an Asian rocery store or online.

1 Peel the ginger and cut into ¼-inch (6 mm) slices.

2 In a small jar, combine the umeboshi vinegar, salt, sugar, mirin, and mustard seeds. Cover and shake to combine.

3 Add the ginger to the jar, cover, and refrigerate for 2 weeks.

4 Remove the ginger slices from the brine and julienne into thin strips.

→ AJITSUKE TAMAGO
(MARINATED HALF-COOKED EGGS) ⇐

Level	**2**
Makes	**6**
Prep Time	1½ hours, plus 2 days to marinate

I try to save time when it comes to cooking in my house, so this recipe is actually two. The ingredients I use to soak my half-cooked eggs in are the same as my mom's recipe for teriyaki sauce. If you want to skip the teriyaki sauce step entirely, that's fine too. The other short cut: if you are making or plan to make Chashu (page 32) or Kakuni (page 36), you can use the braising liquid (about 2 cups, or 480 ml) left over from that recipe to soak your eggs.

Ingredients

1 cup (240 ml) shoyu (soy sauce)

1 cup (200 g) sugar

1½ tsp grated ginger

1 tsp minced garlic

½ cup (120 ml) mirin (sweet rice wine)

6 eggs, at room temperature*

½ cup bonito fish flakes

Eggs should be brought to an even temperature in a warm bath before boiling so that cooking times do not vary. Also, poke a pin-size hole in the bottom of the shells of the eggs for easy peeling later.

1 In a medium saucepan over high heat, whisk together the shoyu, sugar, ginger, and garlic in a medium saucepan. Once the mixture starts bubbling and the sugar dissolves, remove from the heat. Make sure it doesn't bubble over. Stir in the mirin and cool to room temperature or refrigerate for at least 1 hour.

2 Bring a large pot of water to a boil. With a slotted spoon or a Chinese strainer, gently add the eggs to the boiling water, and immediately set a timer for 6½ minutes.

3 While the eggs are cooking, prepare an ice bath for them. When the eggs are done, immediately transfer them to the ice bath. Let them cool in the ice bath for about 10 minutes, then remove the eggs and peel them.

4 In a shallow container that is deep enough for the eggs to be covered in liquid, combine 3 cups (720 ml) water and 1 cup (240 ml) teriyaki sauce, or 1 cup (240 ml) Chashu liquid (see page 32). Add your eggs; cover them with a paper towel by pressing the paper towel down so it's touching the top of the eggs; and pour the bonito fish flakes over the paper towel; the weight of the paper towel will help the eggs marinate on all sides and the bonito flakes will flavor the eggs. Let marinate in the refrigerator for 2 days.

5 Remove the eggs from their soaking liquid and cut each one in half with a very sharp knife.

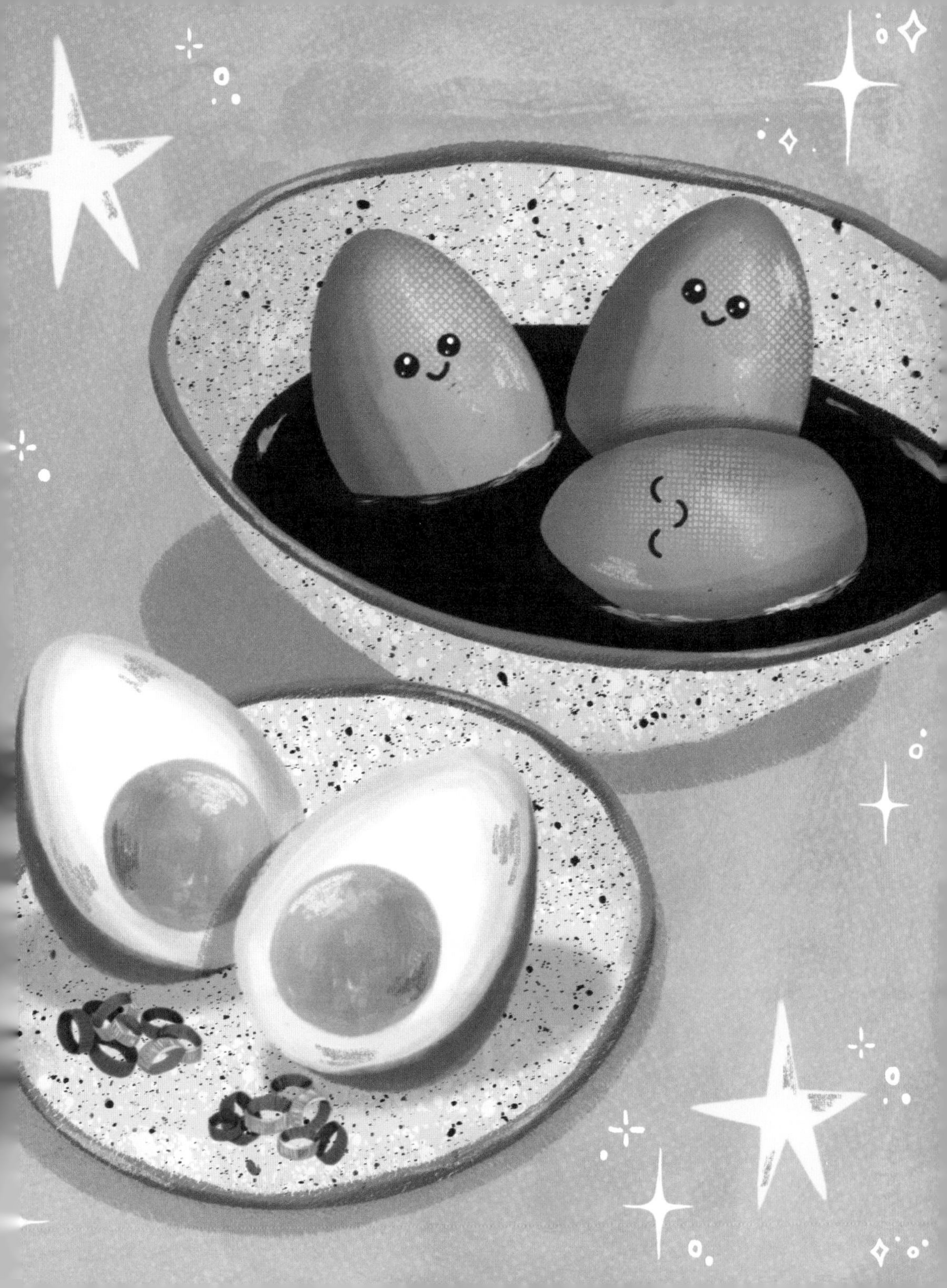

⇥ KAKUNI (BRAISED PORK BELLY) ⇤

Level	2
Serves	6
Prep Time	4 hours cooking time

Kakuni is a pork ramen topping that literally means "square simmered." It's cooked in a fashion similar to Chashu (page 32), but the pork is cut into squares before it is braised. When making kakuni, save the reserved braising liquid. It is a useful ingredient for Ajitsuke Tamago (page 34), or for combining with shiodare to make a very basic Shoyu Base (page 18).

Ingredients

1 lb (455 g) boneless pork belly, cut into large squares

2½ qts or 10 cups (2.8 L) water

1 qt or 4¼ cups (1 L) dark shoyu (soy sauce)

2½ cups (500 g) sugar

¾ cup (180 ml) mirin (sweet rice wine)

1 garlic clove

1 green onion, chopped

1 tbsp grated ginger

1 Combine the pork with the water, shoyu, sugar, mirin, garlic, onion, and ginger in a large pot over high heat. Bring to a boil, reduce to a simmer, and cook until the pork is tender, about 4 hours. Skim off any scum that floats to the surface.

2 Remove the pork from the liquid. Insert a medium-thick wooden skewer into the center of the meat. If it comes out clean, the pork is done.

3 When you are ready to use it, take the pork out of the liquid. Save the liquid for Marinated Half-Cooked Eggs (page 34) or for adding to your Shoyu Base (page 18); do not throw this away! Let the pork rest for at least 2 hours or overnight in the braising liquid in the refrigerator to make it easier to slice (overnight is best as the pork will continue to soak up the juices in that time).

4 Sauté your sliced pork in a skillet for 1 to 2 minutes to render the fat and make the slices crispy before placing on top of ramen. Cut into smaller cubes. Use as many cubes as you'd like to serve on your ramen; typical amounts vary from 1 to 3 pieces

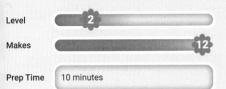

⇒ MAYU (BLACK GARLIC OIL) ⇐

Level 2

Makes 12

Prep Time 10 minutes

Mayu is often used to add depth and flavor to ramen. It's very bitter on its own but mixes well when used in small quantities. Because this recipe requires cooking the garlic until it's charred and completely blackened, I use avocado oil for its high smoke point. Store in a plastic squeeze bottle and drizzle a small amount over the top of the ramen soup before serving.

Ingredients

¼ cup (60 ml) avocado oil

8 garlic cloves, minced

¼ cup (60 ml) sesame oil

1 In a small saucepan over high heat, warm the avocado oil for about 2 minutes. Add the garlic and stir until it turns dark brown. Reduce the heat to medium and continue stirring occasionally until the garlic blackens.

2 Transfer the mixture to a blender and add the sesame oil. Blend on high until well incorporated and smooth.

ROASTED GARLIC BUTTER

Level 2

Serves 4

Prep Time 1 hour 15 minutes

Many ramen shops offer fresh garlic cloves and a press at the table so that you can squeeze the garlic right into your ramen. I prefer the subtler flavor of roasted garlic (plus I don't like sweating garlic all day!). This butter adds flavor and richness to any ramen soup. It's also delicious as a spread on bread or toast.

Ingredients

1 garlic bulb

Salt and black pepper

Olive oil, for drizzling

¼ cup or ½ stick (55 g) unsalted butter, at room temperature

1 Preheat the oven to 400°F (200°C).

2 Cut about ¼ inch (6 mm) off the top of the garlic bulb to expose the tips of the cloves and place the garlic on a piece of aluminum foil.

3 Drizzle the bulb with olive oil, season with salt and pepper, and wrap with the foil to cover completely.

4 Place the wrapped garlic on a cookie sheet. Bake on the center rack for 1 hour, until the bulb starts popping out of its skin and is caramel in color. Feel free to peek in the oven to check.

5 Remove from the oven and let cool for 15 minutes. Break apart the bulb and squeeze the garlic cloves out of their skins onto a cutting board. With the back of a knife or a fork, mash the cloves into a paste.

6 Transfer to a small bowl and combine with the butter until well incorporated. Store in an airtight container and refrigerate for up to 4 weeks. Bring to room temperature before using.

⇒ GARLIC CHIPS ⇐

Level 1

Serves 10

Prep Time 8 minutes

These little flavored chips add just the right texture and balance to the ramen soup. They don't stay crisp for long, though, so prepare them just before you need them.

Ingredients

Extra-virgin olive oil, for frying

garlic cloves, thinly sliced

1 Fill a small saucepan with about ½-inch (13 mm) olive oil and set over medium-high heat. Line a plate with a paper towel.

2 Add a single garlic slice to the hot oil. If it sizzles on contact, you're ready to begin cooking. Add the garlic slices in 2 batches and cook just until lightly browned, 5 to 8 seconds. Watch carefully; these cook very fast and need to be removed promptly, or they will burn and taste very bitter.

3 With a slotted spoon, transfer the cooked garlic chips to the paper towel–lined plate and let cool before serving.

⋛ FRIED ONIONS ⋚

Level 1

Serves 8

Prep Time 10 minutes

These are best when eaten immediately after frying, but they can be stored in an airtight container and reheated in a toaster oven. Serve them as a healthy pile per portion.

Ingredients

2 cups (480 ml) vegetable oil, for frying

1 red onion, halved and thinly sliced, preferably with a mandoline

Salt

1 Fill a large a large heavy-duty skillet with ½-inch (13 mm) oil and set over medium heat. Line a plate with a paper towel.

2 Add an onion slice to the hot oil. If it sizzles on contact, you're ready to fry. Add small batches of onions to the hot oil, taking care that they don't form clumps. Cook until browned and crisp, about 15 seconds. Watch closely; these can burn quickly.

3 With a slotted spoon, transfer the onions to the paper towel-lined plate to cool. Repeat with the remaining batches.

4 Lightly season with salt.

FRIED STRING POTATOES

Level 1

Serves 8

Prep Time 10 minutes

Called *pommes pailles* by the French, these make a delicious topping for ramen. Unlike regular fried potatoes, they stay crisp for hours and you can keep them for up to 3 days—store them in an airtight container and re-crisp them in a toaster oven before use. Serve them as a healthy pile per portion.

Ingredients

2 cups (480 ml) vegetable oil, for frying

1 russet potato, skin on, thinly sliced, preferably with a mandoline

Salt

1 Fill a large heavy-duty skillet with ½-inch (13 mm) oil and set over medium-high heat. Line a plate with a paper towel.

2 Add a potato strip to the hot oil. If it sizzles on contact, you're ready to fry. Add small batches of potatoes to the hot oil and cook until browned and crisp, about 15 seconds. Watch closely; these can burn quickly.

3 With a slotted spoon, transfer the crisped potatoes to the paper-towel–lined plate to cool. Repeat with the remaining batches.

4 Lightly season with salt.

MISO BUTTER

Level 1

Serves 4 (1 tablespoon portions)

Prep Time 5 minutes

Ingredients

¼ cup or ½ stick (55 g) unsalted butter, at room temperature

3 tsp red miso paste

1 In a small bowl, combine the butter and miso paste with a spatula until well incorporated.

2 Store in the refrigerator in an airtight container for up to 2 weeks. Bring to room temperature before use.

PORK, CHICKEN & BEEF RAMEN

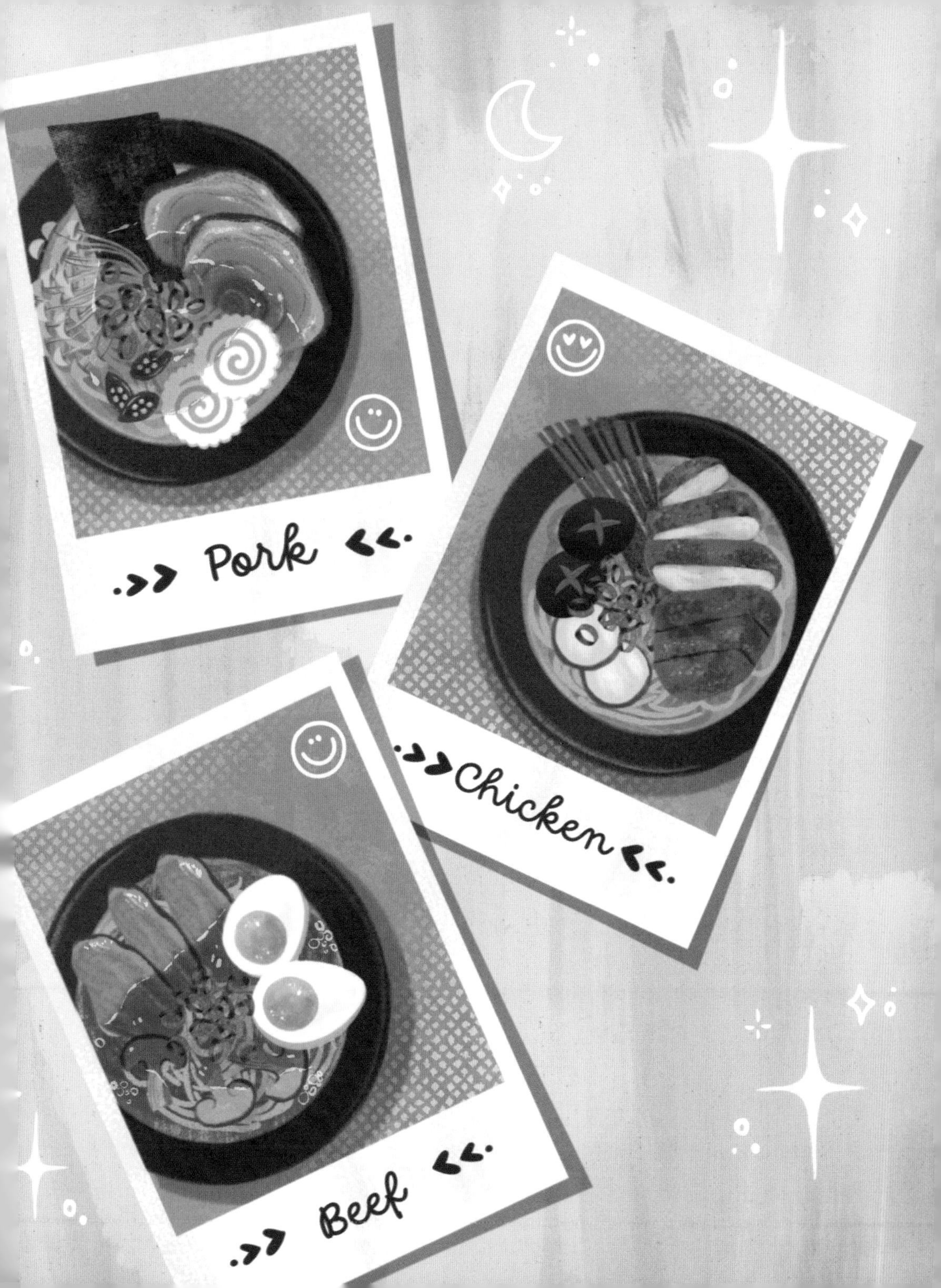
Pork
Chicken
Beef

→ TONKATSU TONKOTSU RAMEN ←

Level **3**

Serves **6**

Prep Time 1 hour, plus time to make the base, noodles (optional), and toppings (optional)

This pork ramen brings together two basic elements of the Japanese kitchen: *tonkatsu*, the breaded and fried cutlets that are so popular as a lunch dish and often included in bento boxes; and *tonkotsu*, the creamy white stock made from long-cooked pork bones, one of the classic bases for ramen.

To Make in Advance

Tonkotsu Base (page 16)

Ramen Noodles (page 24)

Ajitsuke Tamago (page 34)

Menma (page 30)

Ingredients

1½ lbs (670 g) pork tenderloin, cut into ½-inch (13 mm) steaks

Salt and black pepper

½ cup (64 g) cornstarch (I prefer katakuriko, or Japanese potato starch)

2 eggs

1 tbsp water

2 cups (230 g) bread crumbs (I prefer panko)

Vegetable oil, for frying

Additional Toppings

6 green onions, thinly sliced (1 tbsp per serving)

1 bunch bean sprouts (small pile per serving)

1 Season both sides of the tenderloin steaks with salt and pepper.

2 Set up three dipping stations. Spread the cornstarch on a plate. Whisk the eggs and water in a medium-bowl. Pour the bread crumbs on another plate.

3 In a deep, heavy-duty skillet, add about ¾-inch (2 cm) oil. Heat over high to approximately 375ºF (190ºC), or when a little panko sizzles immediately when added.

4 Dip the seasoned pork in each station—cornstarch, then egg, then panko—covering both sides of each piece and shaking off any excess. Set the pork in the skillet and cook for about 2 minutes per side. Remove and set on a paper towel until ready to use. Thinly slice the meat on the diagonal.

5 Boil a pot of water for your noodles. In a separate saucepan, bring 12 cups (2.8 L) tonkotsu base to a boil, then lower the heat and let simmer until it's ready to serve. Right before serving, crank it back up to boil.

6 Boil the noodles (if fresh, boil for about 1 minute; if packaged, boil for about 2 minutes). As soon as they're done, drain well and separate into serving bowls.

7 Pour 2 cups (480 ml) soup over each bowl of noodles. Top each bowl with sliced pork, green onions, bean sprouts, an ajitsuke tamago, and menma.

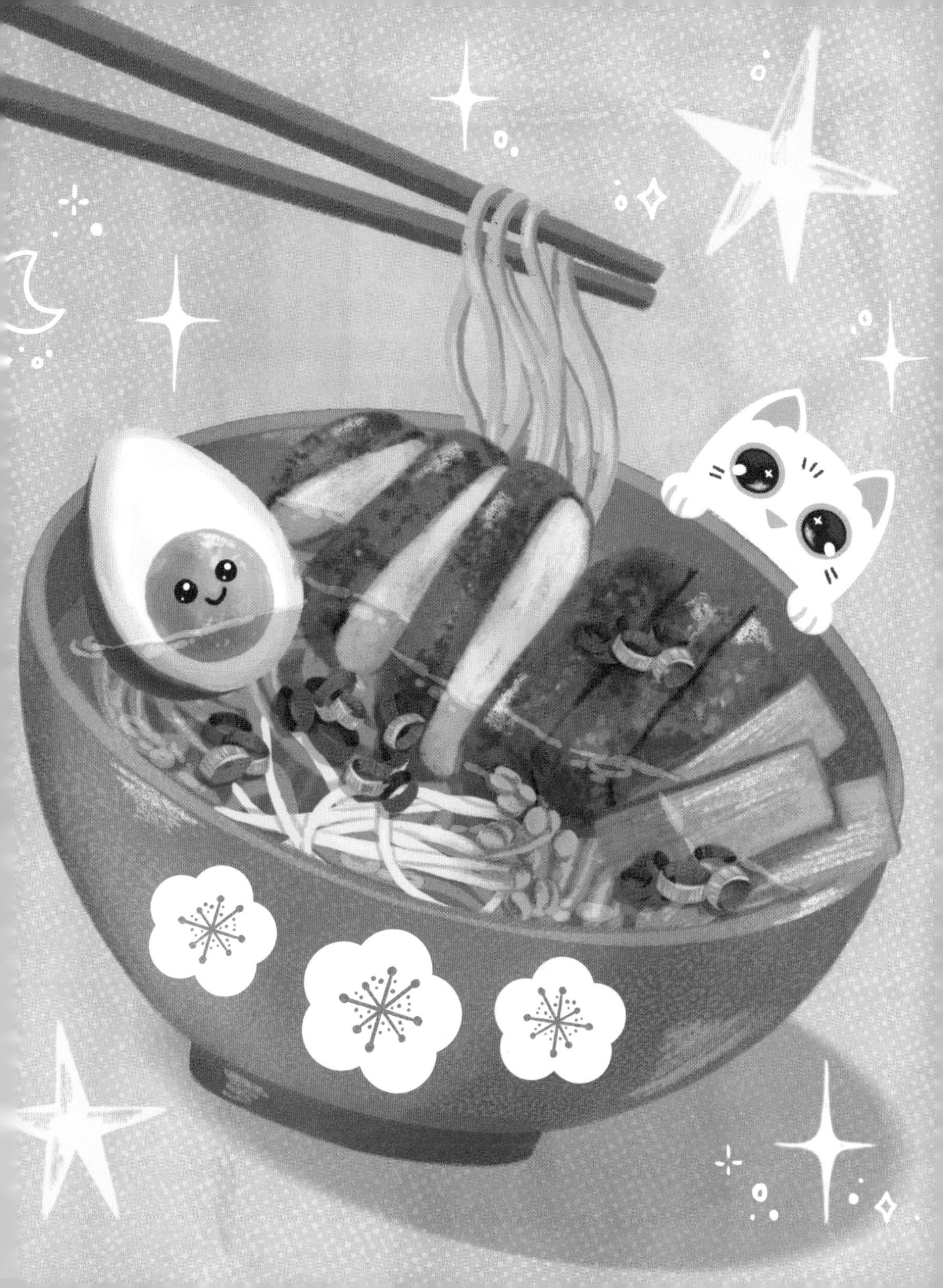

KALUA PORK AND CABBAGE RAMEN

Level	1
Serves	6
Prep Time	5 hours, plus time to make the base and noodles (optional)

I was inspired with this recipe by my Auntie Claudie Naauao, who lives in Hawaii. She suggested that I make a kalua pork version of ramen. I would suggest that you use a slow cooker for this to make it easier.

To Make in Advance

Miso Base (page 14) or your base of choice

Ramen Noodles (page 24)

Ingredients

2 tbsp Hawaiian sea salt

1½ lbs (670 g) pork shoulder

2 tbsp rendered bacon fat (any fat or oil can be substituted)

2 tsp liquid smoke

1 head cabbage (I prefer Napa cabbage), quartered

1 tbsp unsalted butter

2 apples, peeled and diced

1 tsp smoked paprika

Salt and black pepper

12 cups (2.8 L) chicken or vegetable stock

Topping

6 green onions, thinly sliced (1 tbsp per serving)

1 Sprinkle 1 tablespoon sea salt on each side of pork shoulder. In a slow cooker, add the bacon fat, set the pork shoulder on top, and pour the liquid smoke on top. Cover and cook for 3 hours on high. Add the cabbage and continue cooking until meat is tender and shreds easily, about 1 hour longer.

2 Transfer the pork to a cutting board and pull it into shreds with a fork. Transfer the cabbage to a bowl and discard the cooking juices; they will be too salty to use for anything.

3 In a medium skillet over medium-high heat, melt the butter. Add the apples, sprinkle with paprika, and cook, stirring frequently until the apples are tender, about 10 minutes. Remove from the heat and season with salt and pepper.

4 Boil a pot of water for your noodles. In a separate saucepan, bring 2¼ cups (540 ml) miso base and the stock to a boil, then lower the heat and let simmer until it's ready to serve. *Note: It's 3 tablespoons base to 1 cup (240 ml) stock. Right before serving, crank it back up to boil.*

5 Boil the noodles (if fresh, boil for about 1 minute; if packaged, boil for about 2 minutes). As soon as they're done, drain well and separate into serving bowls.

6 Pour 2 cups (480 ml) soup over each bowl of noodles. Top each bowl with a small mound of shredded pork, cabbage, apple, and green onions.

→ INDONESIAN PORK RAMEN ←

WITH COCONUT CURRY SOUP

Level **1**

Serves **6**

Prep Time: 30 minutes cooking, 2 hours marinating, plus time to make the base, noodles (optional), and toppings (optional)

The recipe for the pork marinade in this recipe is from my friend Elisabeth, who was given it by someone she met while hiking in Indonesia. This dish hits all the right flavor notes. I usually marinate the pork overnight to save time.

To Make in Advance

Shio Base (page 20) or your base of choice

Ramen Noodles (page 24)

Tamagoyaki (page 28)

Fried String Potatoes (page 41)

Ingredients

Juice of 1 lime

2 tbsp shoyu (soy sauce)

2 tbsp maple syrup or brown sugar

2 garlic cloves, minced

1 tbsp ground cumin

1 tbsp curry powder

½ tsp sriracha or any chili paste

1 tbsp sesame oil

2 tbsp peanut butter

1½ lbs (670 g) pork tenderloin

1 tbsp unsalted butter

12 cups (2.8 L) chicken or vegetable stock

1½ cups (360 ml) coconut milk (¼ cup, or 60 ml, per serving)

1 tbsp curry powder (½ teaspoon per serving)

3 bananas, sliced on the diagonal

Additional Toppings

bunch cilantro, leaves only (small pile per serving)

lime, cut into 6 segments (1 segment per serving)

1 Set a large zip-top bag in a bowl to keep it steady, then add the lime juice, shoyu, maple syrup or brown sugar, garlic, cumin, curry, Sriracha or other chili paste, sesame oil, and peanut butter. Put the pork loin in the bag, seal it, and move the marinade around so that the pork loins are well coated. Refrigerate and leave to marinate for at least 3 hours or up to 24 hours.

2 Prepare a gas or charcoal grill for medium-high heat. Cook the pork loin over direct heat for about 10 minutes per side, rotating until the internal temperature reaches 145°F (63°C). Transfer the meat to a cutting board and let it rest for at least 8 minutes; the meat should be pink inside.

3 Boil a pot of water for your noodles. In a separate saucepan, bring 2¼ cups (540 ml) shio base and the stock to a boil. Whisk in the coconut milk and curry powder, then reduce the heat and let simmer until ready to serve. *Note: It's 3 tablespoons base to 1 cup (240 ml) stock. Right before serving, crank it back up to a boil.*

4 In a small sauté pan over medium-high heat, cook the butter until it begins to brown. Add the bananas and cook until lightly browned and starting to crisp, about 1 minute on each side.

5 Boil the noodles (if fresh, boil for about 1 minute; if packaged, boil for about 2 minutes). As soon as they're done, drain well and separate into serving bowls.

6 Pour 2 cups (480 ml) soup over each bowl of noodles. Top each bowl with sliced pork, tamagoyaki, fried string potatoes, bananas, a little cilantro, and a segment of lime.

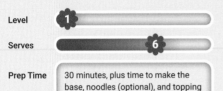
GOOD MORNING RAMEN

Level	1
Serves	6
Prep Time	30 minutes, plus time to make the base, noodles (optional), and topping

Ramen for breakfast, why not? I like to cook bacon in the oven. There's less mess to clean and the bacon ends up perfectly crisp. Just be sure to reserve the bacon fat; you'll need it for many of my basic recipes.

To Make in Advance

Miso Base (page 14) or your base of choice

Ramen Noodles (page 24)

Poached Eggs (page 31)

Ingredients

8 strips bacon (1½ strips per serving)

1 bunch sage leaves

¼ cup or ½ stick (55 g) unsalted butter

12 cups (2.8 L) chicken or vegetable stock

Additional Toppings

1 bunch enoki mushrooms (small pile per serving)

1 avocado, sliced (3 to 4 slices per serving)

1 tomato, diced (small pile per serving)

1 Preheat oven to 400°F (200°C). Lay a piece of parchment paper on a baking sheet. Spread the bacon strips on the sheet and bake for about 20 minutes. Watch carefully as time will vary with ovens. They will crisp up with no need to turn the pieces over. Save your bacon grease in a jar because you can use it to make the ramen soup bases. Remove from the oven and set on a paper towel.

2 Roll the sage leaves into a cigar shape and cut perpendicular to the roll into long strips, or a chiffonade.

3 Heat the butter in a small skillet over high heat until the butter starts to brown. Immediately scatter the sage leaves in the pan and cook for about 10 seconds. Turn the heat off and use a slotted spoon to remove the sage to a paper towel. Keep the browned butter to drizzle over the ramen.

4 Boil a pot of water for your noodles. In a separate saucepan, bring 2¼ cups (540 ml) miso base and the stock to a boil, then lower the heat and let simmer until it's ready to serve. *Note: It's 3 tablespoons base to 1 cup (240 ml) stock. Right before serving, crank it back up to boil.*

5 Boil the noodles (if fresh, boil for about 1 minute; if packaged, boil for about 2 minutes). As soon as they're done, drain well and separate into serving bowls.

6 Pour 2 cups (480 ml) soup over each bowl of noodles. Top each bowl with mushrooms, avocado slices, tomatoes, a poached egg, a crumbled up half strip of bacon, and crispy sage; lay another whole piece of bacon on the side. Drizzle the browned butter over the top for added flavor.

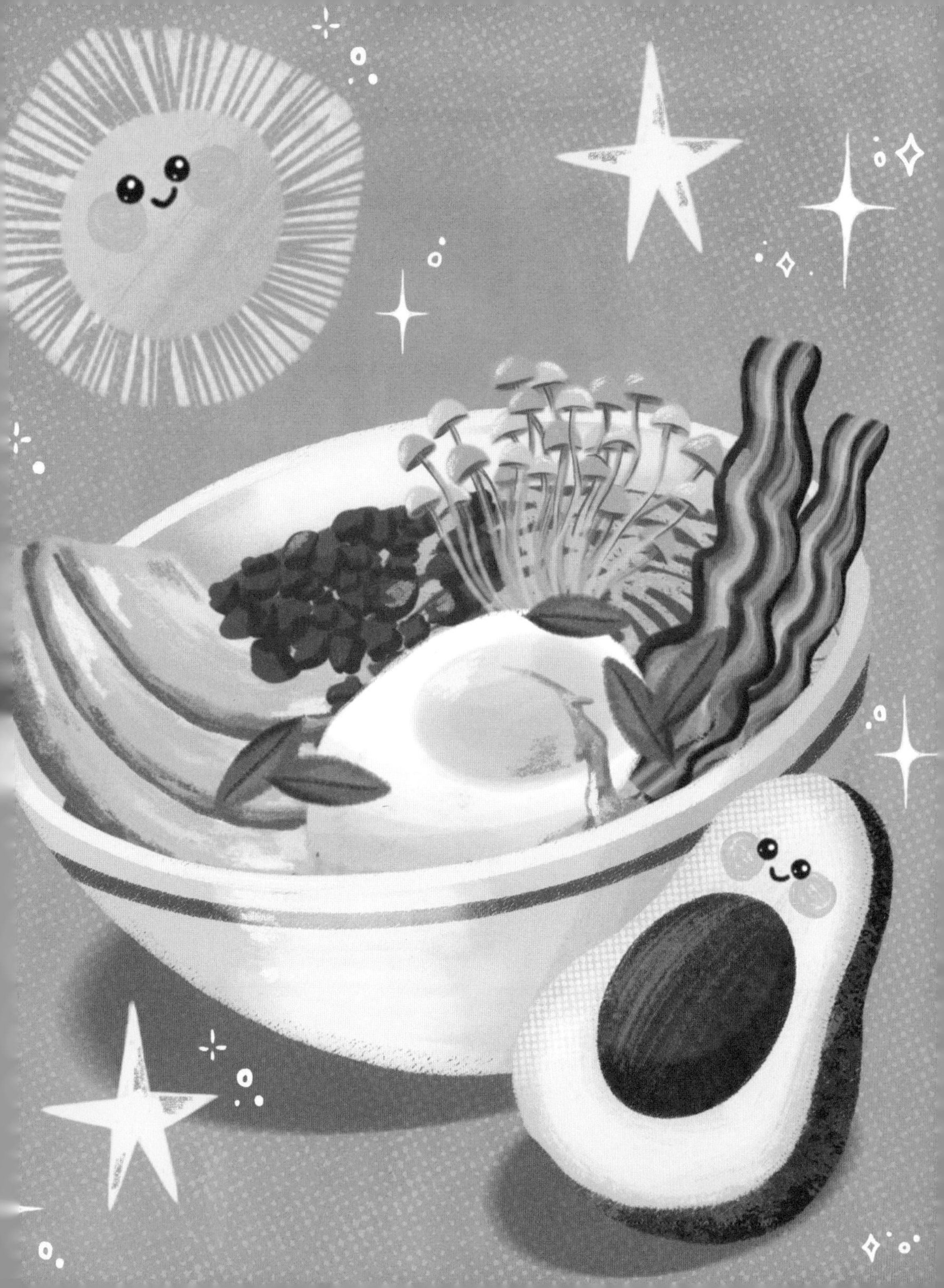

⇥ RANCH-STYLE RAMEN ⇤

Level	2
Serves	6
Prep Time	1 hour, plus time to make the noodles (optional) and topping (optional)

I learned to make this simple clear broth ramen from Sensei Rikisai at the Miyajima Ramen School in Osaka, Japan. It's relatively quick to make compared to more traditional styles of ramen and still has a deep flavor. If you don't have access to kombu, you could substitute wakame, kelp granules, or a teaspoon of fish stock. The flavor will be slightly different, but it will still be delicious!

To Make in Advance

Ramen Noodles (page 24)

Chashu (page 32)

Ingredients

2 lbs (900 g) ground pork, not lean

½ lb (225 g) ground chicken

12 cups (2.8 L) water

4 pieces ginger root (each 2 inches, or 5 cm, long by ½ inch, or 6 mm, wide), skin on, sliced diagonally

4 green onions, thinly sliced (use the green part for soup and white part for topping)

1 large rectangular piece kombu (about 10 inches, or 25 cm, long), cut into large squares

1 large or 2 small dried shiitake mushrooms, crumbled

Salt

Additional Topping

White parts of 4 green onions, thinly sliced, soaked in water for 5 minutes (1 tsp per serving)

1 In a large wok or stockpot, combine the ground pork and chicken with your hands. Add the water, a little at a time, squeezing the meat together and breaking up the fibers and fat until you get a sort of watery mush. You may want to wear disposable gloves to handle the raw meat. Add the ginger, green onions, kombu, and shiitake mushrooms.

2 Turn the heat to high. While the soup is coming to a boil, continue to stir with a large rubber spatula, picking up the mixture from the bottom and swiping the sides so that the meat does not stick. Stir frequently until the mixture comes to a boil and all of the meat has started to cook and the liquid is turning clear. This will take about 10 minutes. After the liquid turns clear, keep at a little bit above a simmer for another 30 minutes.

3 Drain the pork and chicken from the soup—once to get all the larger pieces out with a thicker sieve and again with a very fine sieve to get the remaining pieces out. For the second drain, return the soup to the wok and boil, then turn down to a simmer. Right before serving, crank it back up to a boil.

4 Boil a pot of water for your noodles. Prepare your chashu by frying quickly in a pan on both sides for 1 to 2 minutes to render the fat and make it crispy. Keep it ready to reheat right before placing on top of the ramen.

5 Pour 1½ cups (360 ml) soup into each serving bowl. Season individual bowls with salt, rather than the entire pot, to keep flavors consistent. Season until it's just a bit too salty, because when added to the ramen, the noodles and extra water will take some of the salt taste away and balance it out.

6 Boil the noodles (if fresh, boil for about 1 minute; if packaged, boil for about 2 minutes). As soon as they're done, drain well and separate into the seasoned serving bowls.

7 Squeeze out the excess water from the white parts of the green onions and place a small mound on top. Also add the sliced chashu.

GENG GARI GAI RAMEN

Level: 2

Serves: 6

Prep Time: 45 minutes, plus time to make the base and noodles (optional)

In Thailand, I took a cooking class in which I learned to make the most delicious Geng Gari Gai—a traditional dish from Southern Thailand with aromatic chicken and curry. Though I didn't have access to all the same ingredients that we had in Thailand, I was still able to make this delicious soup.

To Make in Advance

Shio Base (page 20)

Ramen Noodles (page 24)

Ingredients

1 tbsp peanut oil

1 tbsp minced garlic

½ cup (80 g) shallots, chopped 2 dried red chilies

2 cups (240 g) red bell pepper, seeded and chopped into bite-size pieces

2 cups (300 g) Thai eggplant, chopped into bite-size pieces

1½ cups (360 ml) coconut cream

1 tsp salt

¼ tsp white pepper

1 tsp ground turmeric

2 tsp ground coriander

tsp ground cumin

½ tsp ground cloves

tsp grated ginger

tsp lemongrass paste

3 chicken thighs, skin removed, cut into bite-size pieces

2 tbsp fish sauce

Juice of ½ lime (I prefer Kaffir lime)

tbsp brown sugar

13½ cups (3.2 L) chicken stock, divided

Additional Toppings

bunch basil (I prefer Thai basil; 2 sprigs per serving)

½ limes (I prefer Kaffir limes), quartered (1 quarter per serving)

1 Heat the peanut oil in a large skillet or wok over medium-high heat. Add the garlic and shallots and sweat for 2 minutes. Turn heat down to medium and add the chilies, red pepper, and eggplant. Continue to stir for 3 to 4 minutes until the eggplant starts to soften. Remove from the heat and transfer to a bowl.

2 In the same skillet or wok, heat the coconut cream, salt, white pepper, turmeric, coriander, cumin, cloves, ginger, and lemongrass paste over low heat. Season the chicken, add it to the pan, and turn the heat to high. Then reduce the heat to a simmer, cover, and cook for about 15 minutes.

3 Add the fish sauce, juice of ½ lime, brown sugar, and 1½ cups (360 ml) of the stock. Simmer for an additional 10 minutes. Reserve 1 cup (240 ml) of curry sauce from the pan to use separately with your Shio Base. Add the bowl of garlic, shallots, chilies, red pepper, and eggplant to the mixture and continue to simmer until ready to serve.

4 Boil a pot of water for your noodles. In a separate large pot, add the remaining 12 cups (2.8 L) stock, then whisk in 1½ cups (360 ml) shio base, followed by the reserved 1 cup (240 ml) curry sauce. Bring to a boil, then lower the heat and let simmer until ready to use. Right before serving, crank it back up to boil.

5 Boil the noodles (if fresh, boil for about 1 minute; if packaged, boil for about 2 minutes). As soon as they're done, drain well and separate into serving bowls.

6 Pour 2 cups (480 ml) soup over each bowl of noodles. Top with a generous helping of chicken, vegetables, and curry and garnish with basil and a lime segment.

⇒ OVEN-BROILED KARAAGE CURRY RAMEN ⇐

Level	2
Serves	6
Prep Time	1 hour, plus time to make the base, noodles (optional), and toppings (optional)

Karaage is the Japanese version of fried chicken, and I would eat it every day if I could. Since that just wouldn't be healthy, for this recipe, I cheat a bit and bake it in the oven. The chicken ends up wonderfully crisp, and I don't have to deal with a pot of hot oil.

To Make in Advance

Miso Base (page 14) or your base of choice

Ramen Noodles (page 24)

Ajitsuke Tamago (page 34)

Garlic Chips (page 39)

Ingredients

1 cup (240 ml) shoyu (soy sauce)

1 cup (200 g) sugar

1 tsp minced garlic

1 tsp grated ginger

¼ cup (60 ml) mirin (sweet rice wine)

1 lb (455 g) chicken thighs

1 tbsp sesame oil

1 red onion, thinly sliced

12 cups (2.8 L) chicken or vegetable stock

¼ cup (32 g) cornstarch (I prefer katakuriko, or Japanese potato starch)

6 Golden Curry bouillon squares (Japanese store-bought instant curry)

Additional Toppings

1 bunch arugula (I prefer Japanese mizuna lettuce; small pile per serving)

Roasted sesame seeds

3 sheets nori, quartered (2 squares per serving)

1½ lemons, quartered (1 quarter per serving)

1 Add the shoyu, sugar, garlic, and ginger to a small saucepan and bring to boil. Once boiling, remove from the heat and add the mirin. Let cool to room temperature.

2 Pat dry the chicken thighs and cut each piece into bite-size pieces. Add the chicken to a medium bowl and cover with the marinade. Refrigerate and let marinate for at least 1 hour.

3 Heat the sesame oil in a medium skillet over medium-high heat. Add the red onion and sauté until it starts to get charred around the edges. Set aside.

4 Set the oven rack at the top of the oven and preheat the broiler.

5 Drain the excess marinade from the bowl of chicken and sprinkle the chicken with cornstarch until all the pieces are liberally covered. Place the chicken, so that no pieces are touching, on a parchment-lined baking sheet.

6 Broil for about 6 minutes, then flip and broil for an additional 5 minutes, or until they are crispy and brown. Watch closely so they do not burn, as ovens will vary. Set the chicken on a wire rack to cool.

7 Boil a pot of water for your noodles. In a separate saucepan, combine 2¼ cups (540 ml) miso base, the stock, and Golden Curry bouillon squares and bring to a boil. Lower the heat and let simmer until it's ready to serve. Note: It's 3 tablespoons base to 1 cup (240 ml) stock. Right before serving, crank it back up to boil.

8 Boil the noodles (if fresh, boil for about 1 minute; if packaged, boil for about 2 minutes). As soon as they're done, drain well and separate into serving bowls.

9 Pour 2 cups (480 ml) soup over each bowl of noodles. Top with 3 pieces of chicken karaage, sautéed red onions, arugula, an ajitsuke tamago, and garlic chips. Sprinkle with roasted sesame seeds and slip 2 nori squares into the broth. Right before eating, squeeze some lemon juice over the top.

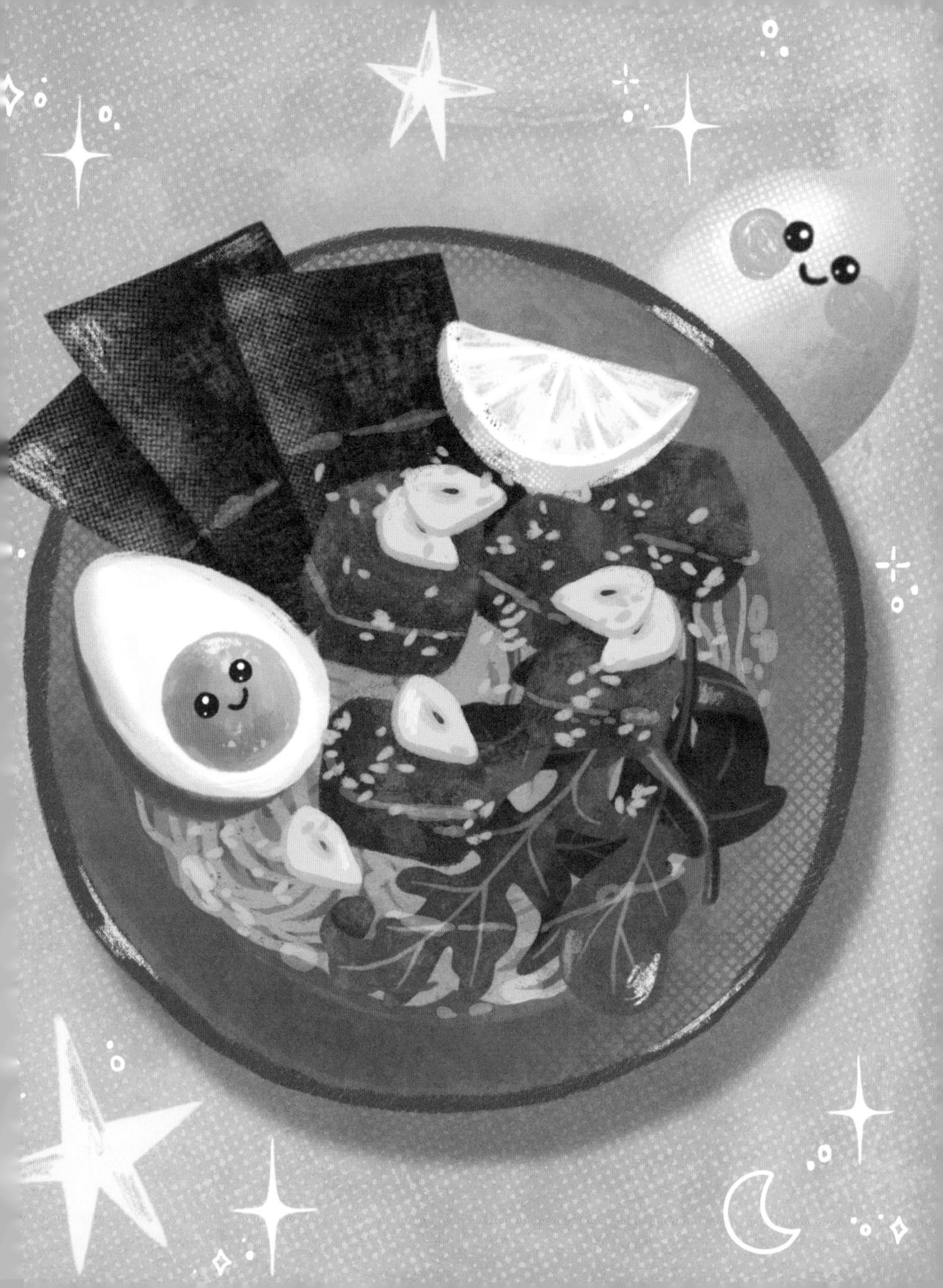

CHICKEN MEATBALL RAMEN

Level	2
Serves	6
Prep Time	40 minutes, plus time to make the base, noodles (optional), and topping (optional)

My husband is Jewish, so I've become pretty familiar with the light texture and fluffiness of a good matzo ball. I wanted to make a chicken meatball that's equally light and delicious, so I borrowed the technique of adding club soda and whipped egg whites to the meat mixture.

To Make in Advance

Shio Base (page 20) or your base of choice

Ramen Noodles (page 34)

Poached Eggs (page 31)

Meatballs

2 egg whites

1 lb (455 g) ground chicken

2 tbsp carrot, finely grated

2 tbsp finely chopped wood ear mushrooms

4 shiso leaves, finely chopped

1 tbsp sugar

1 tbsp shoyu (soy sauce)

¼ cup (60 ml) seltzer or club soda

1 tsp onion powder

½ tsp garlic salt

¼ tsp black pepper

¼ cup (30 g) panko bread crumbs

Broth for Shio Base

12 cups (2.8 L) chicken or vegetable stock

¾ cup or 1½ sticks (175 g) unsalted butter

¾ cup (180 ml) mirin (sweet rice wine)

1 large rectangular piece kombu (about 10 inches, or 25 cm, long), cut into large squares

12 dried shiitake mushrooms

Additional Toppings

1 bunch daikon radish shoots (small pile per serving)

1 red bell pepper, seeded and julienned (¼ cup, or 35 g, per serving)

1 Make the meatballs: Using a mixer or a whisk, whip the egg whites until soft peaks form.

2 In a medium bowl, combine the chicken, carrot, mushrooms, shiso leaves, sugar, shoyu, seltzer, onion powder, garlic salt, and black pepper until well combined. Gently fold in the bread crumbs and the egg whites until just combined. Let the mixture rest for 10 minutes

3 In a large pot, start preparing the broth for your Shio Base. Combine the stock with the butter, mirin, kombu, and mushrooms and bring to a low boil.

4 Make about 24 golf ball–size balls with the chicken mixture, enough for 2 per serving. The trick is to not overhandle the mixture, just gently scoop out and make them as quickly as possible, being careful not to squeeze at all when forming them. With a slotted spoon, drop them right into the stock and cook in batches for about 6 minutes, uncovered.

5 Boil a pot of water for your noodles. Remove the chicken meatballs from your broth, take out the kombu and dried mushrooms and add your 2¼ cups (540 ml) shio base to the broth. *Note: It's 3 tablespoons base to every 1 cup (240 ml) stock. Heat this back up to a boil, then lower the heat and let simmer until ready to use. Right before serving, crank it back up to boil.*

6 Boil the noodles (if fresh, boil for about 1 minute; if packaged, boil for about 2 minutes). As soon as they're done, drain well and separate into serving bowls.

7 Pour 2 cups (480 ml) soup over each bowl of noodles. Top each bowl with 4 meatballs, a small mound of daikon radish shoots, red pepper, and a poached egg.

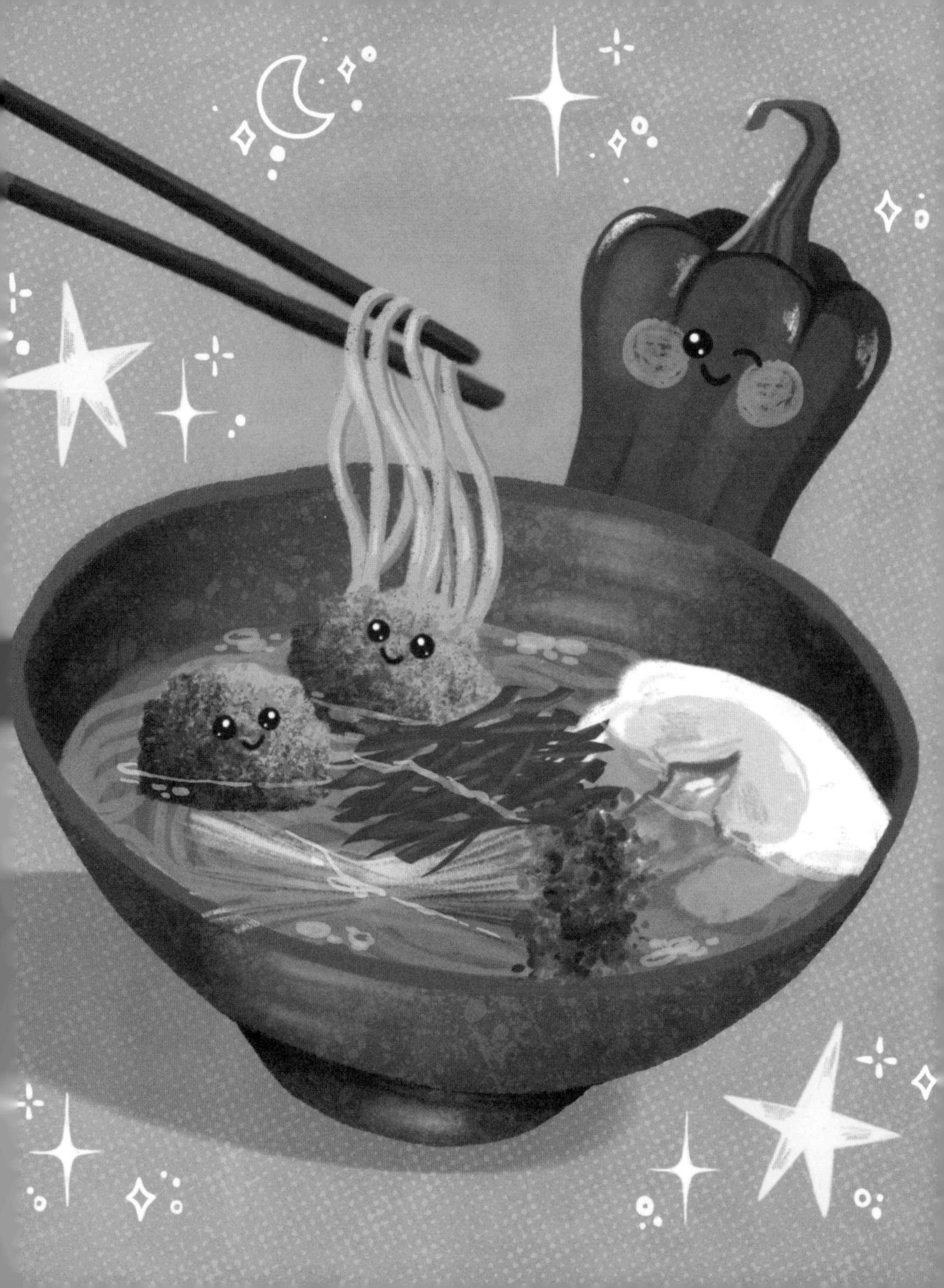

⇒ GREEN SEAWEED FRIED CHICKEN RAMEN ⇐

Level	**3**
Serves	**6**
Prep Time	45 minutes, plus time to make the base, noodles (optional), and topping (optional)

I recently discovered *aonoriko*, a powdered seaweed used to season soups and tempura and as a topping for *okonomiyaki* (a Japanese savory pancake). It's a fine powder and adds dark-green specks of flavor, turning an ordinary batter into something special. This recipe makes an aonoriko-battered chicken that I broil instead of deep-fry, taking on a dumpling-like quality that blends well with ramen.

To Make in Advance

Tonkotsu Base (page 16) or your base of choice

Ramen Noodles (page 24)

Ajitsuke Tamago (page 34)

Chicken

4 tbsp cornstarch (I prefer katakuriko, or Japanese potato starch)

¾ lb (340 g) boneless, skinless chicken thighs, cut into bite-size pieces

1 egg

½ cup (120 ml) cold water

½ cup (55 g) flour

1 tbsp aonoriko (Japanese powdered seaweed)

1 tsp salt

Nonstick cooking spray

Additional Toppings

1 can baby corn (2 or 3 ears per serving)

1 bunch pea shoots (small pile per serving)

6 tsp grated ginger (1 tsp per serving)

1 lemon, sliced into 6 segments

1 Set the oven rack 4 to 6 inches (10 to 15 cm) from the heating element and preheat the broiler.

2 Sprinkle the cornstarch over the chicken pieces.

3 In a separate bowl, whisk the egg, cold water, and flour together. Gently incorporate the aonoriko and salt into the batter without overmixing.

4 Line a cookie sheet with parchment paper and coat with cooking spray so that chicken doesn't stick. Dip the chicken pieces into the batter and lay them on the cookie sheet so that they don't touch.

5 Broil for about 6 minutes, flip, then broil for an additional 5 minutes, or until they start to brown around the edges. Watch closely so they do not burn, as ovens vary. They should resemble the texture of a dumpling. Set the chicken on a wire rack to cool.

6 Boil a pot of water for your noodles. In a separate saucepan, bring 12 cups (1.8 L) tonkotsu base to a boil, then lower the heat and let simmer until you are ready to serve. Right before serving, crank it back up to a boil.

7 Boil the noodles (if fresh, boil for about 1 minute; if packaged, boil for about 2 minutes). As soon as they're done, drain well and separate into serving bowls.

8 Pour 2 cups (480 ml) soup over each bowl of noodles. Top each bowl with a couple pieces of chicken, some baby corn, pea shoots, a mound of spinach, and an ajitsuke tamago. Right before eating, squeeze some lemon juice over the top.

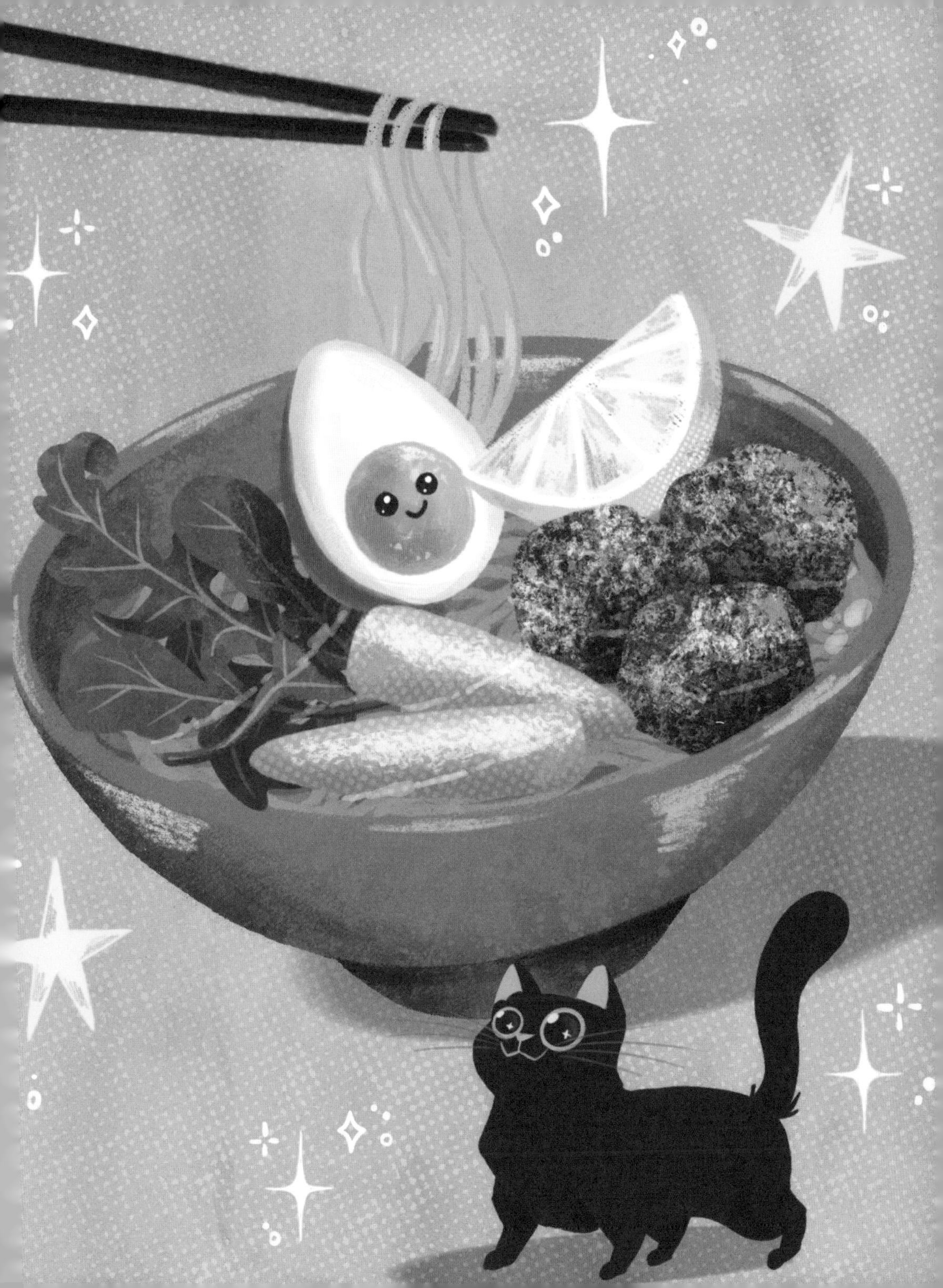

⇥ GINGER CHICKEN RAMEN ⇤

Level	1
Serves	6
Prep Time	45 minutes, plus time to make the base and noodles (optional)

It's definitely not for everyone, but when ginger shines as the star flavor of a dish, I'm a fan. You can increase or reduce the amount as you please, but you know where I stand. It's always easiest to freeze your ginger before grating.

To Make in Advance

Shoyu Base (page 18) or your base of choice

Ramen Noodles (page 24)

Ingredients

2 boneless, skinless chicken breasts, thinly sliced on the diagonal

Salt and black pepper

3 tbsp grated ginger

3 tbsp sake

18 green beans, washed with tips trimmed (3 per serving)

⅓ cup (45 g) cornstarch (I prefer katakuriko, or Japanese potato starch)

3 eggs

1½ tsp shoyu (soy sauce)

1 tsp sugar

1 tbsp unsalted butter

Additional Toppings

2 medium carrots, shredded (2 tbsp per serving)

Roasted sesame seeds

1 Place the sliced chicken into the bottom of a deep medium skillet. Sprinkle the salt, pepper, ginger, and sake over the chicken. Cover with a drop lid or aluminum foil with a small hole in the center. Bring to a boil, then lower to a simmer and cook about 8 minutes, or until liquid starts to evaporate.

2 Remove the chicken and set in a bowl. Let it cool and finely shred it. Keep the shredded chicken in the juices from the bowl until ready to serve.

3 In the same skillet used above, heat ¼-inch (6 mm) vegetable on medium-high.

4 In a shallow dish, dredge the green beans in the cornstarch ur well coated. Fry the green beans in batches in the oil on both side until golden brown. Remove and set on a paper towel.

5 Boil a pot of water for your noodles. In a separate saucepan, bring 12 cups (2.8 L) shoyu base to a boil, then lower the heat an let simmer until it's ready to serve. Right before serving, crank it back up to boil.

6 Right before you are about to pour the soup in your bowls, yo need to make your shoyu egg scramble. In a small bowl, combin the eggs, shoyu, and sugar. Beat well.

7 Heat 1 tablespoon butter in a medium skillet over high heat. When the butter starts to brown, pour in your beaten eggs and very quickly mix around with chopsticks. When the eggs are bare cooked, remove from the pan and set in a bowl; they should be somewhat runny.

8 Boil the noodles (if fresh, boil for about 1 minute; if packaged boil for about 2 minutes.) As soon as they're done, drain well and separate into serving bowls.

9 Pour 2 cups (480 ml) soup over each bowl of noodles. Top ea bowl with a large mound of shredded ginger chicken, shredded carrots, shoyu egg scramble, and roasted sesame seeds.

⇴ KOBE BEEF TSUKEMEN ⇴

Level 1

Serves 4

Prep Time 45 minutes, plus time to make the base, noodles (optional), and topping (optional)

Kobe beef, the delicious and tender well-marbled beef from Kobe, a city in Japan's Hyogo prefecture, isn't exactly something you find at your grocery store every day, but when you do stumble across it, treat yourself to something divine. Look out for the pieces of Kobe that come with a little square of beef suet, or beef fat. You can melt the suet and sear the meat in it for additional flavor and umami.

To Make in Advance

Shoyu Base (page 18) or your base of choice

Ramen Noodles (page 24)

Roasted Garlic Butter (page 38)

Ingredients

1 tbsp fresh lemon juice (I prefer Meyer lemons)

1 tbsp shoyu (soy sauce)

1 tbsp sake

1 tbsp mirin (sweet rice wine)

2 Kobe beef steaks or any well-marbled beef

Salt and black pepper

1 tbsp beef suet (beef fat that you can ask your butcher for)

⅓ cup (43 g) grated fresh horseradish

Additional Toppings

4 raw quail eggs

¼ cup (30 g) grated daikon (small mound per serving)

4 shiso leaves (1 leaf per serving)

4 lemon (1 thin slice per serving)

1 In a small bowl, whisk the lemon juice, shoyu, sake, and mirin to make a marinade. Sprinkle the steak with salt and pepper.

2 Melt the suet in a medium skillet over high heat. Add the steak and quickly sear on both sides, until just cooked, leaving the meat rare in the center. Add the marinade to coat and remove the steak from the pan to rest, leaving the juices in the pan. Reduce the marinade and pan juices for about 1 minute in the skillet.

3 Boil a pot of water for your noodles. In a separate saucepan, bring 4 cups (946 ml) shoyu base to a boil. Add the remaining cooking marinade and pan juices from the steak, whisk in the horseradish, and then lower the heat and let simmer until it's ready to serve. Right before serving, crank it back up to boil.

4 Cut the steak into small squares; the meat should be on the rare to medium-rare side.

5 Boil the noodles (if fresh, boil for about 1 minute; if packaged, boil for about 2 minutes). As soon as they're done, drain well and separate into serving bowls.

6 Add half of one cubed steak to the serving bowls. Top with a quail egg, mound of daikon, a shiso leaf, a thin slice of lemon, and a dollop of roasted garlic butter. Serve the soup, 1 cup, or 240 ml, per serving in a separate bowl for dipping.

SUKIYAKI RAMEN

Level	1
Serves	4
Prep Time	30 minutes, plus time to make the base, noodles (optional), and toppings (optional)

I love everything about *sukiyaki*—traditionally wafer-thin beef, served hot-pot style by simmering with vegetables, tofu, and a jelly-type noodle, and often dipped in raw egg. Here, I've added quail eggs as a topping, in case you find a raw egg is too much. It cooks really quickly, so just make sure you have all of your other components ready to go.

To Make in Advance

Miso Base (page 14) or your base of choice

Ramen Noodles (page 24)

Fried Onions (page 40)

Black Garlic Oil (page 37)

Ingredients

½ cup (120 ml) shoyu (soy sauce)

½ cup (100g) sugar

¼ cup (60 ml) mirin (sweet rice wine)

2 tbsp sake

1 tsp minced garlic

1 tsp grated ginger

1 medium carrot, cut into matchsticks

¼ cup (30 g) julienned daikon radish

½ cup (75 g) julienned red bell pepper

½ cup (35 g) shredded cabbage (I prefer Napa cabbage)

4 mushrooms (I prefer shiitake mushrooms), thinly sliced

1 block medium-firm tofu, cut into bite-size cubes

1 lb (455 g) sukiyaki beef or paper-thin slices of beef

Salt and black pepper

8 cups or 2 qts (2 L) chicken or vegetable stock

Additional Topping

4 green onions (1 tbsp per serving), sliced diagonally

8 raw quail eggs (optional)

1 Make the cooking liquid by whisking the shoyu, sugar, mirin, sake, garlic, and ginger together until combined.

2 Warm the liquid in a medium skillet over a high heat. When it reaches a boil, turn down to medium-high heat and add the carrot, daikon radish, red pepper, cabbage, and mushrooms. Cook for 5 minutes, then remove with a slotted spoon and set aside. Next, cook the tofu for an additional 5 minutes. Remove it and set aside.

3 Season the beef with salt and pepper, then add it and cook it very quickly. Leave it as rare as possible; the heat of the ramen soup will continue to cook it, so it's okay if it's redder than is usually safe. Remove it and set aside.

4 Boil a pot of water for your noodles. In a separate saucepan, bring 1½ cups (360 ml) miso base and the stock to a boil. Add the remaining cooking liquid from the sukiyaki to your soup base, then lower the heat and let simmer until it's ready to serve. *Note: It's 3 tablespoons base to 1 cup (240 ml) stock. Right before serving, crank it back up to boil.*

5 Boil the noodles (if fresh, boil for about 1 minute; if packaged, boil for about 2 minutes). As soon as they're done, drain well and separate into serving bowls.

6 Pour 2 cups (480 ml) soup over each bowl of noodles. Top each bowl with 3 or 4 pieces of sukiyaki meat, a pile of vegetables, a pile of tofu, green onions, 2 quail eggs, and fried onions and drizzle black garlic oil over the soup.

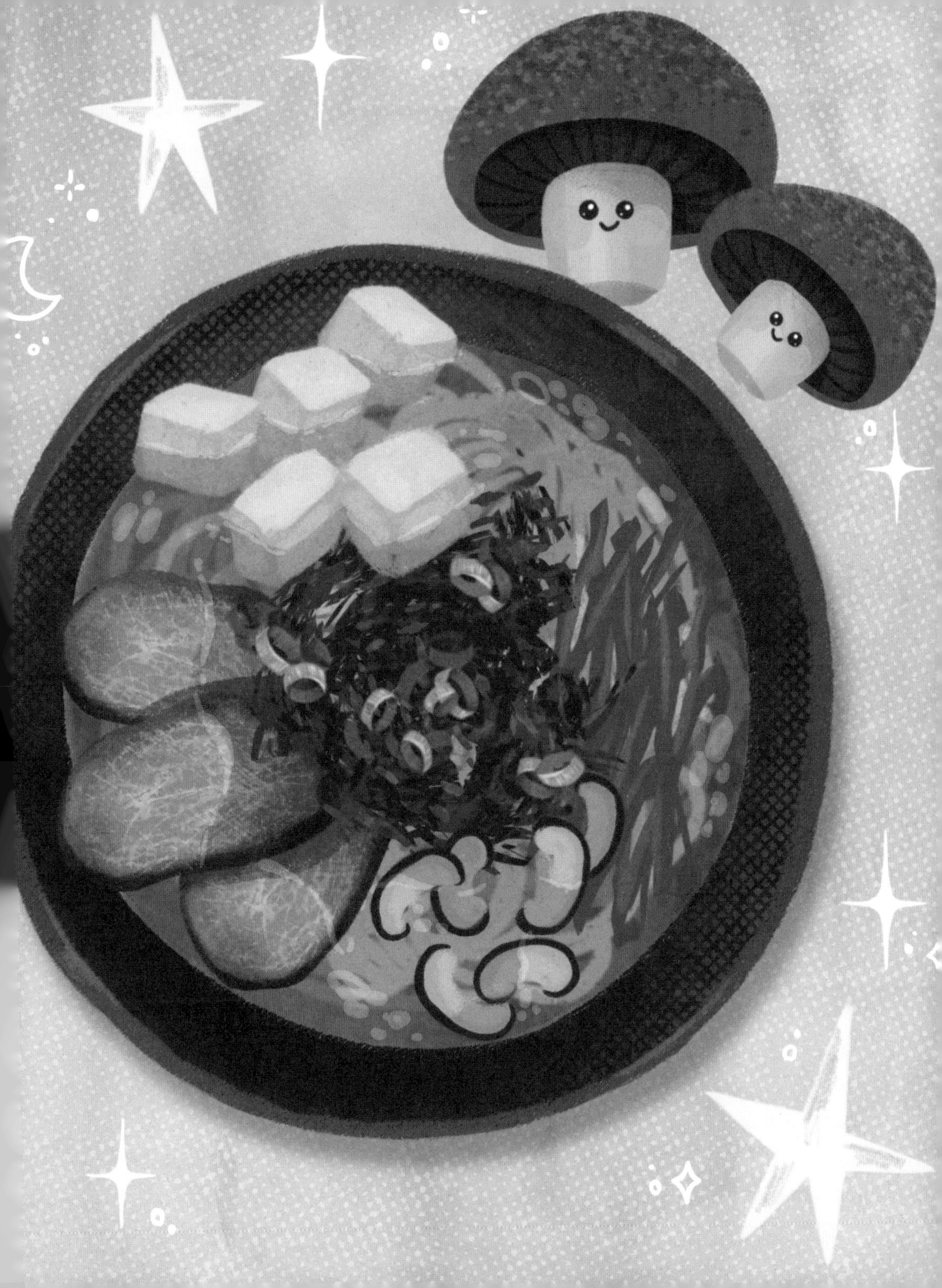

→ TERIYAKI BEEF-WRAPPED ASPARAGUS RAMEN ←

Level	2
Serves	6
Prep Time	30 minutes, plus time to make the base, noodles (optional), and toppings (optional)

When I was a kid, my mom made beef-wrapped asparagus appetizers whenever she hosted fancy parties. Now, I think they're the perfect addition to elevate any ramen. You can add any fresh vegetables that you feel would complement this ramen as well.

To Make in Advance

Miso Base (page 14) or your base of choice

Ramen Noodles (page 24)

Fried String Potatoes (page 41)

Ajitsuke Tamago (page 34)

Ingredients

½ lb (225 g) thinly sliced beef sirloin (I prefer shabu shabu beef)

½ lb (225 g) asparagus spears, trimmed

4 tbsp shoyu (soy sauce)

4 tbsp sugar

1 tbsp grated ginger

½ tsp minced garlic

2 tsp sesame oil

½ lb (225 g) baby bok choy, rinsed and dried (substitute Swiss chard)

Sea salt

12 cups (2.8 L) chicken or vegetable stock

Additional Toppings

1½ small tomatoes (I prefer Momotaro tomatoes, sliced into eighths) (2 slices per serving)

3 sheets nori, quartered (2 squares per serving)

Roasted sesame seeds

1 Cut the raw beef slices in half and roll each asparagus spear in a half slice of beef, pressing the meat around asparagus so that it is tightly rolled and stays secure.

2 In a small bowl, combine the shoyu, sugar, ginger, and garlic. Whisk to combine.

3 Heat 1 teaspoon sesame oil in a large skillet over medium-high heat. Add the rolled beef and asparagus and cook for about 5 minutes, turning throughout until all sides are lightly browned. Pour the sauce mixture over the beef and asparagus and turn to coat. Remove and set onto a plate, then pour the remaining sauce over the top. When cool, slice each spear in half diagonally.

4 In the same skillet you used to brown the beef and asparagus, heat 1 teaspoon of sesame oil over high heat. Add the bok choy and quickly cook on both sides until tender, about 2 minutes. Remove and season with a sprinkle of sea salt.

5 Boil a pot of water for your noodles. In a separate saucepan, bring 2¼ (540 ml) cups miso base and the stock to a boil, then lower the heat and let simmer until it's ready to serve. *Note: It's 3 tablespoons base to 1 cup (240 ml) stock. Right before serving, crank it back up to a boil.*

6 Boil the noodles (if fresh, boil for about 1 minute; if packaged, boil for about 2 minutes). As soon as they're done, drain well and separate into serving bowls.

7 Pour 2 cups (480 ml) soup over each bowl of noodles. Top each bowl with 4 halved slices of beef-wrapped asparagus, a small bunch of bok choy, 2 tomato slices, a pile of fried string potatoes, and an ajitsuke tamago. Tuck 2 squares of nori into the soup, then sprinkle some roasted sesame seeds.

SEAFOOD RAMEN

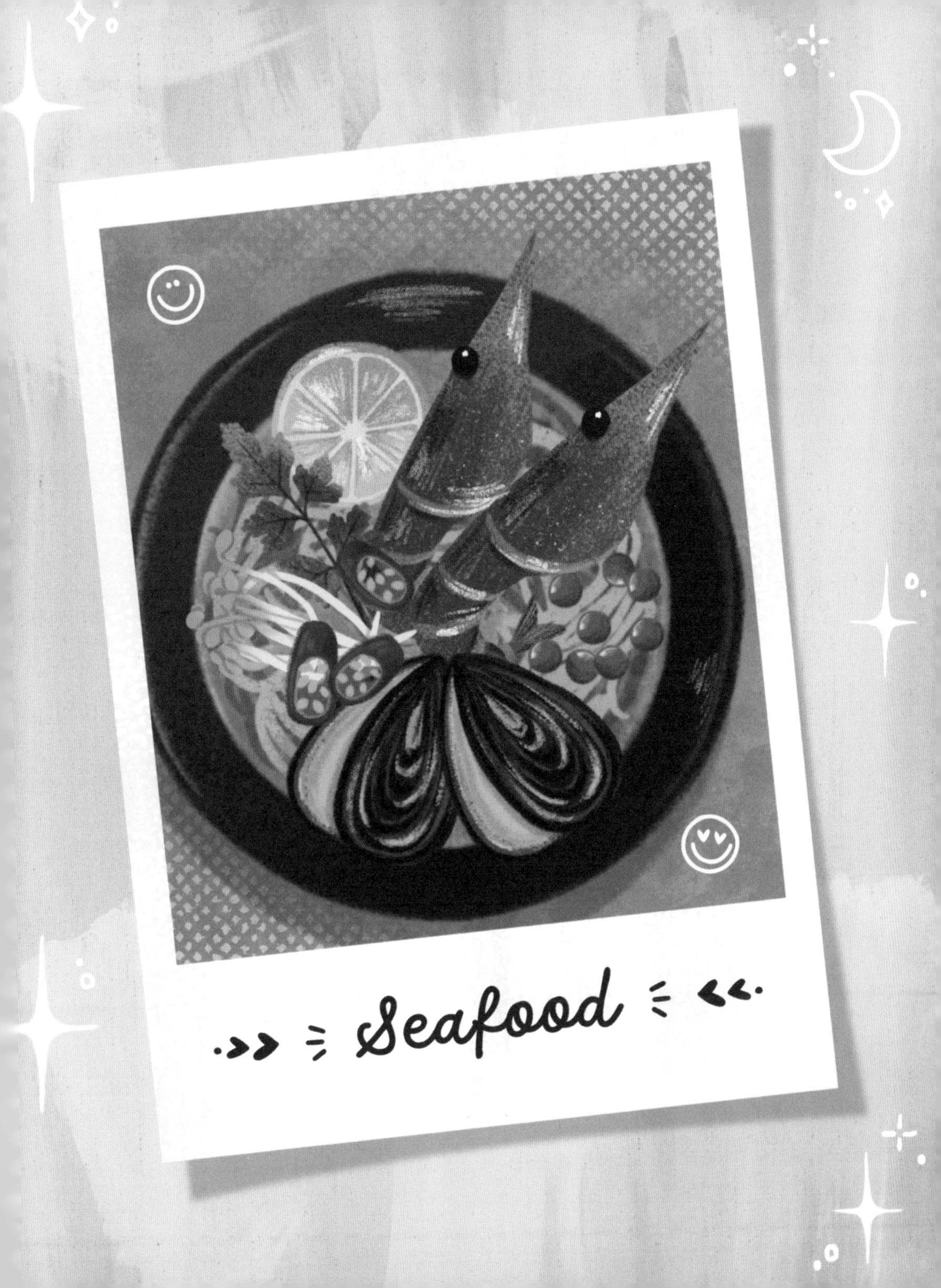
Seafood

⇒ CRISPY SOFT-SHELL CRAB RAMEN ⇐

Level	2
Serves	6
Prep Time	1 hour, plus time to make the base, noodles (optional), and toppings (optional)

I like to cook the soft-shell crabs under the broiler and have found that as long as you remove and press out any excess water from the crabs before dredging them with *katakuriko*, or cornstarch, they cook up perfectly golden.

To Make in Advance

Shoyu Base (page 18) or your base of choice

Ramen Noodles (page 24)

Ajitsuke Tamago (page 34)

Roasted Garlic Butter (page 38)

Soft-Shell Crabs

6 whole soft-shell crabs

¼ cup (32 g) cornstarch (I prefer katakuriko, or Japanese potato starch)

Nonstick cooking spray

Toppings

3 sheets nori, quartered (2 squares per serving)

¼ lb (340 g) fresh spinach (2 oz, or 55 g, per serving)

1 avocado, sliced (3 or 4 slices per serving)

1 bunch enoki mushrooms (small pile per serving)

1 cup (240 ml) yuzu citrus juice (substitute lime juice, 2 tbsp per serving)

1 Set the oven rack 4 to 6 inches (10 to 15 cm) from the heating element and preheat the broiler.

2 Gently squeeze out any water from the soft-shell crabs and dab lightly with a paper towel. Lightly dredge the soft-shell crabs on both sides with cornstarch and place on a lined cookie sheet. Spray the crabs with nonstick cooking spray on both sides. Broil for about 5 minutes, then flip and broil for an additional 5 minutes, or until they are crispy and brown. Watch closely so they do not burn, as ovens will vary.

3 Boil a pot of water for your noodles. In a separate saucepan, bring 12 cups (2.8 L) shoyu base to a boil, then lower the heat and let simmer until it's ready to serve. Right before serving, crank it back up to a boil.

4 Boil the noodles (if fresh, boil for about 1 minute; if packaged, boil for about 2 minutes). As soon as they're done, drain well and separate into serving bowls.

5 Pour 2 cups (480 ml) soup over each bowl of noodles. Slip 2 nori squares into the broth of each bowl and top with soft-shell crab, spinach, avocado slices, mushrooms, 2 tablespoons lime juice, an ajitsuke tamago, and a scoop of roasted garlic butter.

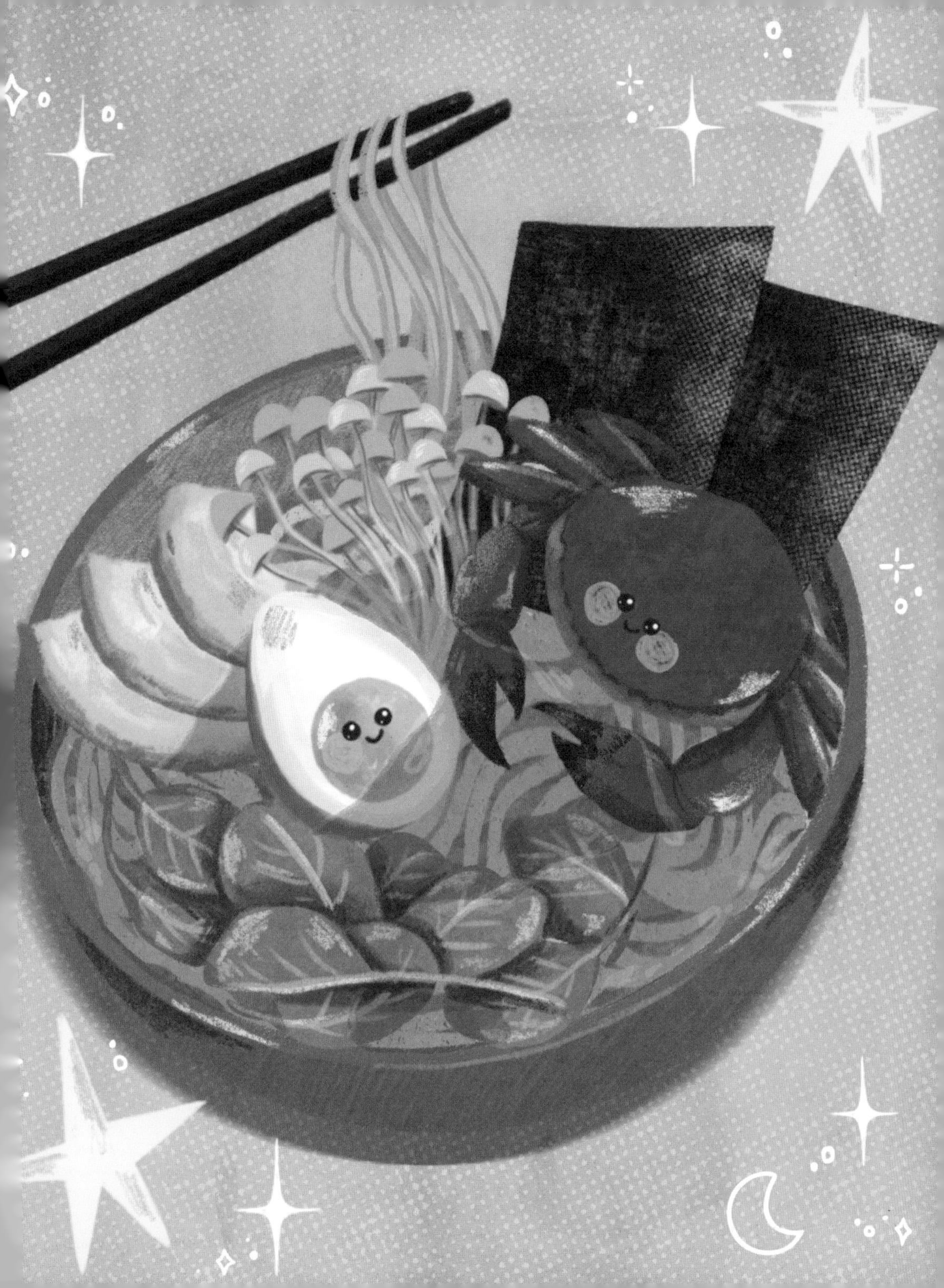

� MALAYSIAN CURRY LAKSA RAMEN ⇇

Level	3	
Serves	4	
Prep Time	1 hour, plus time to make the base and noodles (optional)	

This recipe was created by my friend Emily Lai, which is a staple of Malaysian cuisine and stems from the basic ingredients of fresh roots and coconut milk. It shouldn't be too difficult to find dried shrimp; just look for fresh ones that are bright pink, coral-colored, and whole, as opposed to brown and falling apart.

To Make in Advance

Shio Base (page 20) or your base of choice
Ramen Noodles (page 24)

Ingredients

1½-inch (4 cm) piece turmeric or 1 tbsp turmeric powder

1½-inch (4 cm) piece ginger root (I prefer galangal), chopped

3 medium shallots, chopped

8 garlic cloves, chopped

15 dried chilies, seeds removed and soaked in hot water for 20 minutes

5 red chilies, chopped

4 cashews (I prefer candlenuts)

1½ oz (40 g) dried shrimp

1 tbsp ground coriander

1 lemongrass, white part only, chopped

1½ quarts (1.7 L) water

Pinch of salt, plus more if needed

1 chicken breast

1 lb (455 g) shrimp, peeled and halved lengthwise, with shells reserved (if shrimp have heads, also reserve)

4 tbsp vegetable oil

1 can (13.5 oz, or 400 ml) coconut milk

¼ lb (115 g) mung bean sprouts

Toppings

2 hard-boiled eggs, peeled and halved (½ egg per serving)

¼ lb (115 g) green beans, cut into bite-size pieces and blanched (1 oz, or 28 g, per serving)

1 red chili (I prefer Fresno chillies), sliced (1 tsp per serving)

1 handful mint leaves (small bunch per serving)

1 lime, quartered (1 wedge per serving)

1 Prepare the laksa paste by blending the turmeric, ginger, shallots, garlic, dried chilies, red chilies, cashews, dried shrimp, coriander, and lemongrass together in a food processor or blender until it turns into a paste.

2 In a medium pot with a lid, bring the water and a pinch of salt to a boil. Add the chicken breast, and when the water returns to a boil, cover and let the chicken steep in the hot water for 20 minutes. Do not open the lid.

3 Remove the chicken then return the water to a boil and add the shrimp. Cook for 5 minutes, then remove and let cool. Add reserved shrimp shells and heads to the cooking liquid. Let simmer for 10 minutes, then strain out all solids. Add ¾ cup (180 ml) shio base and let simmer for another 10 minutes.

4 Boil a large pot of water for your noodles. Heat the oil in a large skillet over medium-high heat. Add the laksa paste and sauté until the oil starts to separate. Reserve a few tablespoons for your topping. Add the coconut milk to your shio soup infused with chicken and shrimp and bring it to a boil. Check for seasoning to see if more salt needs to be added.

5 Blanch the mung bean sprouts in the same ramen noodle water for 30 seconds and set aside. Boil the noodles (if fresh, boil for about 1 minute; if packaged, boil for about 2 minutes). As soon as they're done, drain well and separate into serving bowls.

6 Pour 2 cups (480 ml) soup over each bowl of noodles. Top with bean sprouts, a hard-boiled egg, green beans, chili, mint, and a spoonful of the reserved laksa paste. Garnish with a lime wedge. If desired, top with chicken and shrimp meat.

⇀ SOUTHERN CRAWFISH RAMEN ↽

Level	3
Serves	4
Prep Time	1 hour, plus time to make the base and noodles (optional)

Another great recipe that Emily Lai and I developed together! We had so much fun experimenting with different combinations for this Louisiana-style ramen.

To Make in Advance

Shoyu Base (page 18) or your base of choice

Ramen Noodles (page 24)

Ingredients

2 lbs (900 g) cooked crawfish with shells and heads (langostinos or shell-on shrimp can be substituted)

2½ quarts (2.8 L) water

½ cup (150 g) salt

1 tsp black pepper

1 tsp ground coriander

1 tsp ground cloves

2 tsp cayenne

2 tsp paprika

1 tsp oregano

1 tsp thyme

1 whole lemon, halved

1 whole sweet onion, peeled and sliced

4 whole garlic cloves, smashed

2 tbsp vegetable oil, divided

1 small onion, chopped

1 red bell pepper, seeded and chopped

2 celery ribs, chopped

6 oz (170 g) smoked sausage (I prefer andouille), sliced ¼ inch (6 mm) thick

Toppings

4 green onions, sliced diagonally (1tbsp per serving)

Zest of 4 lemons (1 tsp per serving)

tsp gumbo file powder, optional (¼ tsp per serving)

1 De-shell the crawfish, saving the shells and setting the meat and heads aside for topping the soup. Fill a large pot with the water and add the crawfish shells, salt, black pepper, coriander, cloves, cayenne, paprika, oregano, thyme, lemon (squeeze in juice and add halves), onion, and garlic. Bring to a boil over high heat for about 30 minutes. Save the stock for later use.

2 Heat 1 tablespoon oil in a large saucepan over medium-high heat. Add the onion, bell pepper, and celery (or what is called the "holy trinity") and let sweat for 10 minutes. Place in a bowl and set aside.

3 In the same saucepan used above, heat 1 tablespoon vegetable oil over medium-high heat. Add the sliced sausage and cook through, turning throughout, for about 5 minutes until browned.

4 Boil a pot of water for your noodles. In a separate large saucepan, combine 5 cups (1.2 L) shoyu base with 3 cups (720 ml) crawfish shell stock and 1½ cups (360 ml) holy trinity (step 2) and bring to a boil. Lower the heat and let simmer until you are ready to serve. Right before serving, crank it back up to a boil.

5 Boil the noodles (if fresh, boil for about 1 minute; if packaged, boil for about 2 minutes). As soon as they're done, drain well and separate into serving bowls.

6 Pour 2 cups (480 ml) soup over each bowl of noodles. Top each bowl with a small pile of crawfish meat, holy trinity, sausage, green onions, lemon zest, and a sprinkle of file powder. Garnish with a crawfish head.

EGG DROP RAMEN

Level	3
Serves	4
Prep Time	30 minutes, plus time to make the base and noodles (optional)

My friend Emily Lai generously shared her method for making traditional egg drop soup as the base for this ramen. She published the original in *Vogue* magazine, so this is something special.

To Make in Advance

Shio Base (page 20) or your base of choice

Ramen Noodles (page 24)

Ingredients

8 cups or 2 qts (2 L) chicken stock

1 ham hock or ½ lb (225 g) smoked sausage or bacon

¼ lb (115 g) Napa cabbage, roughly chopped

Salt

1 lb (455 g) sea bass, skin removed, cut into 4 portions

1 tsp sesame oil

¼ lb (115 g) snap peas

4 eggs

4 tsp Shaoxing wine (substitute sake or dry sherry)

Toppings

¼ lb (115 g) Napa cabbage, julienned (1 oz, or 28 g, per serving)

2 oz (55 g) wood ear mushrooms (½ oz, or 15 g, per serving)

Zest of 4 lemons (1 tsp per serving)

1 In a large pot, bring the stock, 1½ cups (360 ml) shio base, the ham hock, and cabbage to a boil. Simmer for 1 hour so that the soup can absorb the flavors of the ham hock and cabbage.

2 Lightly salt both sides of the sea bass and immerse in the soup. Cook for 5 to 7 minutes to poach. Remove the fish and set aside. Strain the ham hock and the cabbage out of the soup and discard. Bring the liquid to a boil, then lower the heat and let simmer until you are ready to serve.

3 Boil a pot of water for your noodles. Heat the sesame oil in medium skillet and sauté the snap peas for about 2 minutes. Sprinkle with salt and remove from the heat.

4 In a small bowl, whisk the eggs and Shaoxing wine together.

5 Boil the noodles (if fresh, boil for about 1 minute; if packaged, boil for about 2 minutes). As soon as they're done, drain well and separate into serving bowls.

6 Crank the heat up on the soup base to boil, turn off the heat and immediately whisk in the egg mixture with a chopstick. You'll see the eggs cook and create light strings throughout the soup.

7 Pour 2 cups (480 ml) soup over each bowl of noodles. Top each bowl with a portion of sea bass, snap peas, a pile of julienned cabbage, mushrooms, and lemon zest.

→ FURIKAKE SALMON RAMEN ←

Level	1
Serves	6
Prep Time	30 minutes, plus time to make the base, noodles (optional), and topping (optional)

This recipe is great because if you don't have the ramen soup base or fresh ramen noodles ready, you can eat the salmon on its own with some rice and a vegetable. I happen to love the salmon on ramen because the *furikake* adds an additional crunchy texture and flavor.

To Make in Advance

Shoyu Base (page 18) or your base of choice

Ramen Noodles (page 24)

Ajitsuke Tamago (page 34)

Furikake Salmon

1½ lbs (680 g) salmon fillet, skin on (ask for the thickest part)

¼ cup (60 g) mayonnaise (I prefer Kewpie mayo)

1 tbsp shoyu (soy sauce)

1 tsp sesame oil (I prefer the Kadoya brand because it is very strong)

¼ cup (26 g) furikake (Japanese condiment made from sesame seeds, seaweed, and salt)

Toppings

1½ cups (105 g) julienned mushrooms (I prefer shiitake; ¼ cup, or 17 g, per serving)

¾ cup (40 g) chopped chives (2 tbsp per serving)

1½ lemons, quartered (1 quarter per serving)

1 Set the oven to broil. Place the salmon, skin side down, on a baking sheet lined with foil or a nonstick liner. In a small bowl, whisk together the mayonnaise, shoyu, and sesame oil. Using a spatula, evenly spread the mixture in a thin layer over the salmon. Evenly sprinkle the furikake over the salmon to lightly coat it.

2 Broil the salmon for about 8 minutes, or until just done; this varies depending on the thickness of the fillet (do not overcook). Remove from the broiler and slice into 4 even portions, about 1½ inches (4 cm) wide. Remove the salmon skin.

3 Boil a pot of water for your noodles. In a separate saucepan, bring 12 cups (2.8 L) shoyu base to a boil, then lower the heat and let simmer until it's ready to serve. Right before serving, crank it back up to boil.

4 Boil the noodles (if fresh, boil for about 1 minute; if packaged, boil for about 2 minutes). As soon as they're done, drain well and separate into serving bowls.

5 Pour 2 cups (480 ml) soup over each bowl of noodles. Top with a portion of furikake salmon, mushrooms, chives, and an ajitsuke tamago. Squeeze the lemon over right before eating.

⇢ SWEET CHILI SALMON RAMEN ⇠

Level	2
Serves	6
Prep Time	20 minutes, plus time to make the base, noodles (optional), and toppings (optional)

The salmon on its own is one of my mom's favorite dishes, which I make for her every time she visits. I thought it would be great on ramen because the extra-crispy salmon skin gives it texture and it goes well with broccoli and broccolini.

To Make in Advance

Shoyu Base (page 18) or your base of choice

Menma (page 30)

Ramen Noodles (page 24)

Roasted Garlic Butter (page 38)

Ingredients

6 oz (170 g) salmon fillet, skin on (1 oz, or 28 g, per serving)

Salt and black pepper

2 tsp vegetable oil, divided

1 bunch broccoli (substitute broccolini), diced

4 tbsp shoyu (soy sauce)

2 tbsp sweet chili sauce

1 tbsp sesame oil

1 Lightly season both sides of the salmon fillet.

2 Heat 1 teaspoon of vegetable oil in a medium skillet over medium-high heat. Add the broccoli, sprinkle with salt and pepper, and sauté for about 1 minute per side, then add 3 tablespoons of water and cover to let steam for an additional 2 minutes. Remove and set aside.

3 To the same pan, heat 1 teaspoon of vegetable oil in a medium skillet over medium-high heat. Add the salmon, skin side down, and cover to steam for about 6 minutes, or until the salmon flesh just turns opaque. Remove the salmon and lay it skin side up on a cutting board. Gently remove the skin by running a knife along the underside of the skin and the salmon and return the skin to the pan. Fry it over high heat on both sides for about 2 minutes until it gets crispy. Remove and set on a paper towel.

4 To the same pan, add the shoyu, sweet chili sauce, and sesame oil and combine over medium heat until the sauce bubbles. Right before serving, return the salmon fillets to the pan and turn them in the sauce until completely covered.

5 Boil a pot of water for your noodles. In a separate saucepan, bring 12 cups (2.8 L) of shoyu base to a boil, then reduce the heat and let simmer until you are ready to serve. Right before serving, crank it back up to a boil.

6 Cut the fried salmon skin into small strips and set aside.

7 Boil the noodles (if fresh, boil for about 1 minute; if packaged, boil for about 2 minutes). As soon as they're done, drain well and separate into serving bowls.

8 Pour 2 cups (480 ml) of soup over each bowl of noodles. Top each bowl with a fillet of cooked salmon, a couple of branches of broccoli, a small mound of menma, and a dollop of garlic butter. Sprinkle the fried salmon-skin strips on top.

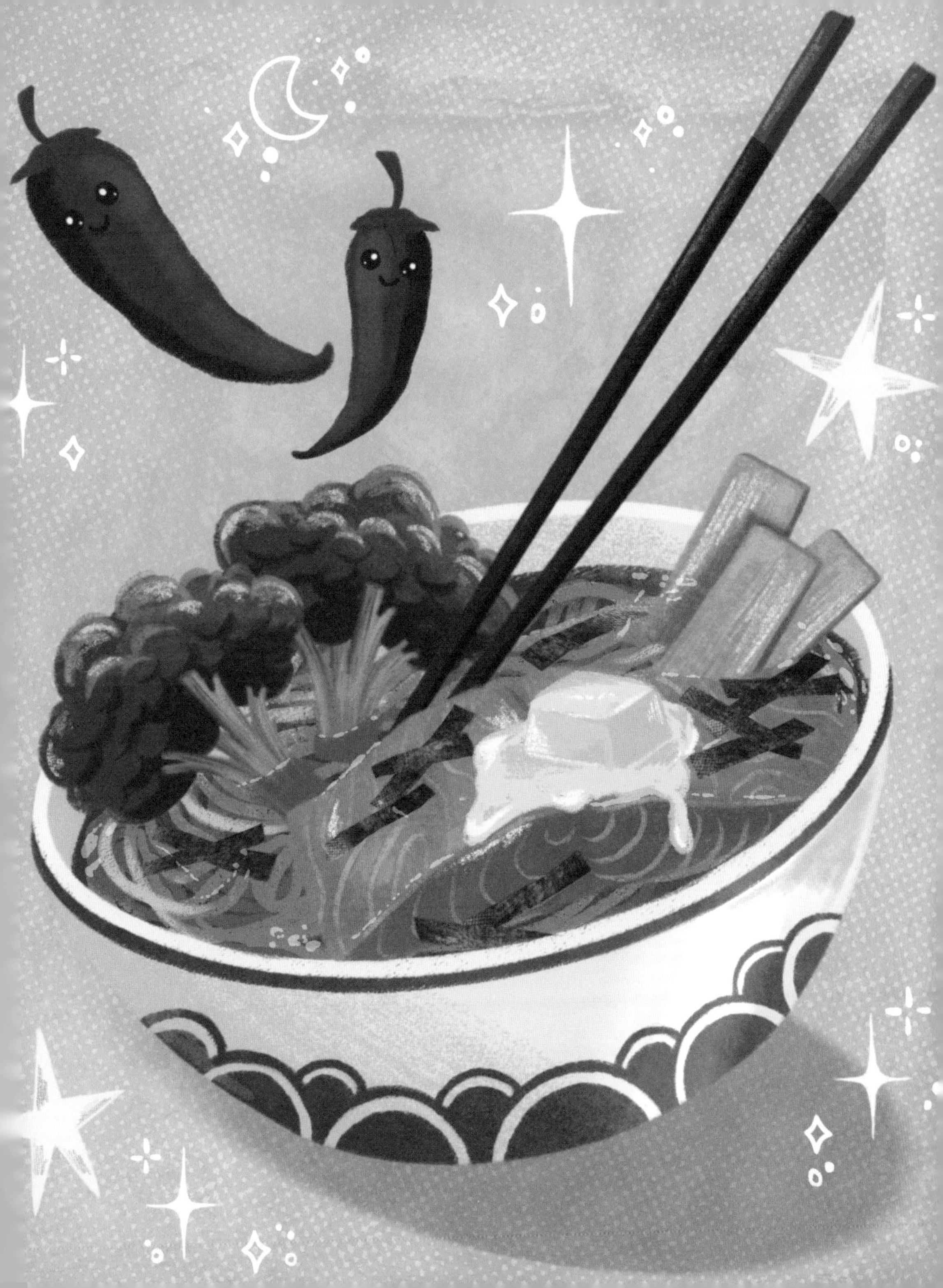

⇢ CALIFORNIA RAMEN ⇠

Level	2
Serves	6
Prep Time	20 minutes, plus more to make the base, noodles (optional), and topping (optional)

Being a California native, I love the fresh, accessible ingredients found in a California roll. During crab season, our family always eats a ton of fresh Dungeness crabs, and if you have access to any, this recipe is pretty simple to pull together. Most grocery stores carry cooked Alaskan king crab legs that you can take home and crack open—no fuss.

To Make in Advance

Shoyu Base (page 18) or your base of choice

Ramen Noodles (page 24)

Ajitsuke Tamago (page 34)

Ingredients

2 lbs (900 g) cooked fresh crab (I prefer Dungeness)

1 tsp olive oil

¾ cup or 1½ sticks (170 g) unsalted butter

6 tsp minced garlic

½ lemon

Additional Toppings

1 cucumber, julienned (small bunch per serving)

1 avocado, sliced (couple slices per serving)

3 green onions, thinly sliced (½ tbsp per serving)

1 lemon, cut into 6 segments (1 segment per serving)

2 sheets nori, sliced into 6 pieces (2 pieces per serving)

Shichimi togarashi (Japanese mixed chili pepper spice), optional

1 Crack the crab and set aside.

2 Boil a pot of water for your noodles. In a separate saucepan, bring 12 cups (2.8 L) shoyu base to a boil, then lower the heat and let it simmer until it's ready to serve. Right before serving, crank it back up to a boil.

3 In a small saucepan, heat the olive oil and butter, then add the garlic and squeeze the lemon over it. Cook until just sizzling.

4 Boil the noodles (if fresh, boil for about 1 minute; if packaged, boil for about 2 minutes). As soon as they're done, drain well and separate into serving bowls.

5 Pour 2 cups (480 ml) soup over each bowl of noodles. Top with cracked crab, cucumber, avocado, green onion, and an ajitsuke tamago. Drizzle the garlic butter over the crab and sprinkle shichimi togarashi on the avocado. Tuck the nori into the soup. If you want to warm your crab, put a handful in a small sieve and heat it in the noodle water for 10 seconds before adding it.

⇥ LOBSTER RAMEN ⇤

Level 3

Serves 6

Prep Time 45 minutes, plus time to make the base, noodles (optional), and topping (optional)

Equipment Wooden skewers, soaked in water for at least 15 minutes

This one hits it out of the park—the lobster shell–infused Shio Base is amazing, and it is also very pleasing to the eye—with the shredded purple cabbage adding such beautiful color and the lemon zest giving a brightness to both the soup and the lobster.

To Make in Advance

Shio Base (page 20)

Ramen Noodles (page 24)

Roasted Garlic Butter (page 38)

Lobster

6 lobster tails, 5 to 6 oz (140 to 170 g) each

6 tbsp clarified butter (I prefer ghee)

Lobster Broth

12 cups (2.8 L) chicken or vegetable stock

¾ cup or 1½ sticks (170 g) unsalted butter

¾ cup (180 ml) mirin (sweet rice wine)

1 large rectangular piece of kombu (about 10 inches, or 25 cm, long), cut into large squares

2 dried shiitake mushrooms, crumbled into small pieces

4 bay leaves

Additional Toppings

½ head red cabbage, shredded (small mound per serving)

1 bunch arugula and spinach mixed (small mound per serving)

1½ lemons, quartered (¼ tsp zest and 1 quarter per serving)

1 Preheat oven to 450°F (230°C).

2 Split the lobster tails down the center of the back by turning over and cutting in half lengthwise through the shell with kitchen scissors, starting from the top and leaving the fin intact. Thread a soaked skewer through the underside of the tail through the bottom of the shell.

3 Brush the underside portion with the exposed meat with clarified butter. Wrap in foil and set on a baking tray. Bake for 15 minutes. Remove the lobster tails from the foil and reserve the drippings.

4 In a large stockpot over a high heat, combine the stock, butter, mirin, kombu, dried shiitake mushrooms, bay leaves, and reserved lobster drippings. Bring to a boil and reduce to a simmer.

5 Carefully remove the lobster meat from the shell by sliding a knife under the meat and gently lifting it out of its shell. Add the shells and the lobster juices to your stock. Cover and simmer for about 30 minutes.

6 Boil a pot of water for your noodles. Line a colander with cheesecloth and set it over a pot large enough to hold the stock. Strain the lobster stock and return it to the stove. Add ¾ cup (180 ml) shio base. Right before serving, crank it back up to a boil.

7 Boil the noodles (if fresh, boil for about 1 minute; if packaged, boil for about 2 minutes). As soon as they're done, drain well and separate into serving bowls.

8 Pour 2 cups (480 ml) soup over each bowl of noodles. Top each bowl with a lobster tail, shredded purple cabbage, and a small mound of arugula-spinach mix. Add the lemon zest and a dollop of roasted garlic butter and squeeze a lemon wedge over each bowl before serving.

VEGETABLE RAMEN

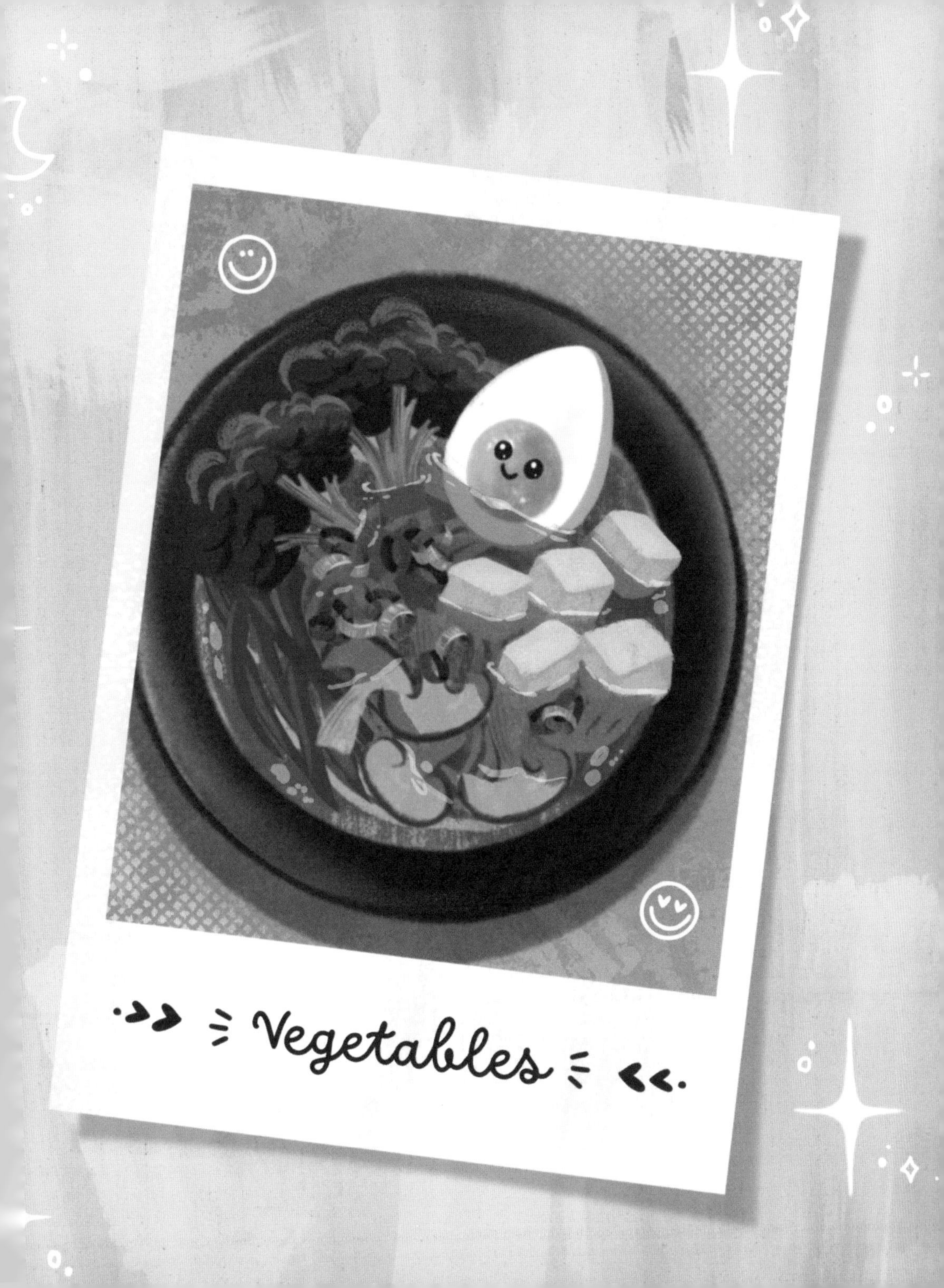
Vegetables

→ KABOCHA RAMEN ←

Level	3
Serves	6
Prep Time	1 hour, plus time to make the base, noodles (optional), and toppings (optional)

Kabocha has a rich and nutty flavor, and because the skin is edible when cooked, there's no peeling required. In this ramen, the bitterness and spice of the mizuna lettuce balances the sweetness of the squash. The fried shiso leaf gives it a surprise crunch to start your first bite.

To Make in Advance

Shoyu Base (page 18)

Ramen Noodles (page 24)

Ajitsuke Tamago (page 34)

Roasted Garlic Butter (page 38)

Kabocha

½ medium kabocha (Japanese squash)

2 tbsp shoyu (soy sauce)

1 tsp salt

½ tsp dashi granules

½ cup (100 g) sugar

¼ cup (60 ml) mirin (sweet rice wine)

1 cup (240 ml) water

Tempura Batter

1 egg

1 cup (240 ml) cold water

1¼ cups (155 g) all-purpose flour, sifted

Vegetable oil, for frying

6 shiso leaves

Additional Toppings

1 bunch buna shimeji mushrooms (small mound per serving)

1 bunch arugula (I prefer mizuna lettuce; small bunch per serving)

1 Cut the kabocha in half and remove the seeds with a spoon. Save one half for later. Cut the stem and bottom off the remaining half and cut into 1½-inch (4 cm) cubes. No need to take the skin off.

2 In a medium skillet, whisk the shoyu, salt, dashi, sugar, mirin, and water. Bring to a boil and then reduce to simmer. Add the kabocha in one layer so that each piece is touching the sauce; the sauce should almost cover the kabocha. Simmer, uncovered, until the kabocha is soft, approximately 45 minutes. Turn each piece over halfway through cooking. When finished, the liquid should be almost gone.

3 Make a tempura batter out of the egg, cold water, and flour. Add ½-inch (13 mm) oil to a medium skillet over medium-high heat. Dip the shiso leave(s) into the batter mixture one at a time. When a little flour thrown in starts to sizzle, fry the shiso leaves for 10 seconds per side, making sure they do not touch each other in the pan. Set on a paper towel to remove excess oil.

4 Boil a pot of water for your noodles. In a separate saucepan, bring 12 cups (1.8 L) shoyu base to a boil, then lower the heat and let simmer until you are ready to serve. Right before serving crank it back up to a boil.

5 Boil the noodles (if fresh, boil for about 1 minute; if packaged, boil for about 2 minutes). As soon as they're done, drain well and separate into serving bowls.

6 Pour 2 cups (480 ml) soup over each bowl of noodles. Top each bowl with kabocha, a shisho leaf, mushrooms, arugula, an ajitsuke tamago, and 1 tablespoon of roasted garlic butter.

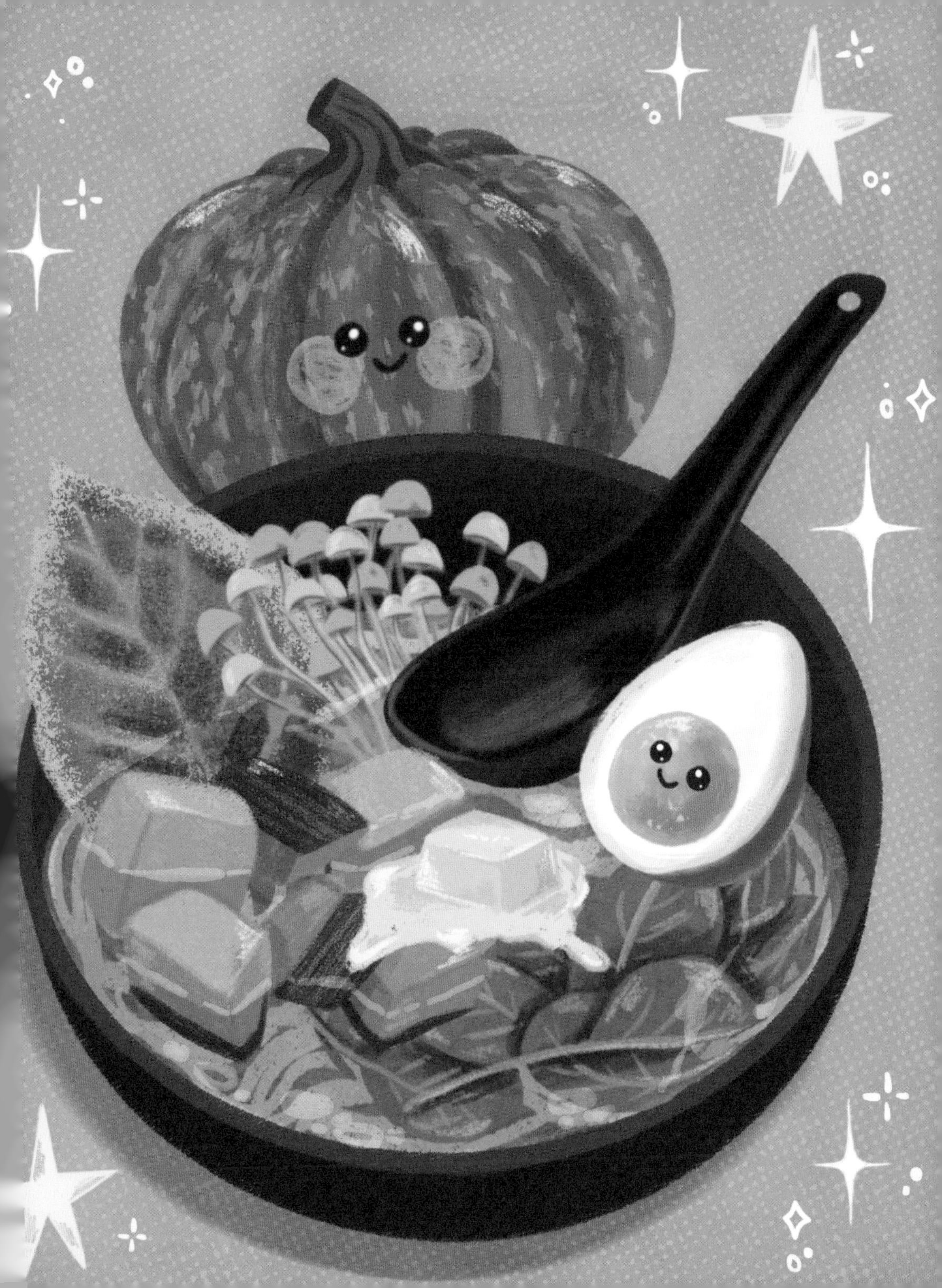

⇀ SIMMERED NASUBI RAMEN ⇁

Level	2
Serves	4
Prep Time	30 minutes, plus time to make the base, noodles (optional), and toppings (optional)

My mom always served *nasubi*, or Japanese eggplant, in the most appealing way, leaving the stem intact and slicing through the flesh so that it fanned out on the plate. I love this presentation of the eggplant and red cabbage on top of ramen, with its purple hues.

To Make in Advance

Tonkotsu Base (page 16) or your base of choice

Ramen Noodles (page 24)

Tamagoyaki (page 28)

Miso Butter (page 41)

Eggplants

4 Japanese eggplants

Salt and black pepper

2 tbsp shoyu (soy sauce)

2 tbsp mirin (sweet rice wine)

1 tbsp rice wine vinegar

1 tsp sugar

1 tsp sesame oil

Additional Toppings

½ head red cabbage, shredded (small mound per serving)

1 tsp grated ginger (½ tsp per serving)

2 green onions, thinly sliced (1 tsp per serving)

1 Cut the eggplants lengthwise in ¼-inch (6 mm) strips, leaving the stems intact so that they can fan out. Lightly season both sides with salt and pepper.

2 In a small bowl, combine the shoyu, mirin, rice wine vinegar, and sugar. Whisk to combine.

3 Heat the sesame oil in a large skillet over medium-high heat. Add the eggplants, working in batches, fanning each one out so that they are lying flat and none are touching. Cook for about 3 minutes on each side, or until they are lightly browned and the meat has softened.

4 Add all the eggplant back into the skillet and pour sauce over them, turning to evenly coat. Remove the eggplant and set on a plate and pour the remaining sauce over the top.

5 Boil a pot of water for your noodles. In a separate saucepan, bring 8 cups (1.8 L) tonkotsu base to a boil, then lower the heat and let simmer until it's ready to serve. Right before serving, crank it back up to boil.

6 Boil the noodles (if fresh, boil for about 1 minute; if packaged, boil for about 2 minutes). As soon as they're done, drain well and separate into serving bowls.

7 Pour 2 cups (480 ml) soup over each bowl of noodles. Top each bowl with 1 fanned eggplant, a mound of red cabbage, grated ginger, green onion, tamagoyaki, and miso butter.

⇾ MUSHROOM-LOVER'S RAMEN ⇽

Level	**2**
Serves	**4**
Prep Time	1 hour, plus time to make the base, noodles (optional), and topping (optional)

With so many Japanese mushrooms to choose from, just go with whatever is fresh for the season. The only mushrooms I wouldn't recommend here are matsutake mushrooms because of their high cost and strong flavor. Any other mushroom varieties works, so pick four of your favorites.

To Make in Advance

Shio Base (page 20) or your base of choice

Ramen Noodles (page 24)

Ajitsuke Tamago (page 34)

Ingredients

¼ lb (115 g) forest nameko mushrooms, divided

¼ lb (115 g) buna shimeji mushrooms, divided

¼ lb (115 g) enoki mushrooms, divided

¼ lb (115 g) shiitake mushrooms, divided

8 cups or 2 qts (2 L) chicken or vegetable stock

1 cup (230 g) heavy whipping cream

2 chicken bouillon cubes

1 tsp shichimi togarashi (Japanese mixed chili pepper spice), optional

Additional Toppings

¼ head red cabbage, shredded (small mound per serving)

4 tsp grated ginger (1 tsp per serving)

4 green onions, thinly sliced (1 tbsp per serving)

1 Pulse half of each of the mushrooms in a food processor until finely chopped; if you don't have a food processor, you can finely chop them by hand. The remaining mushrooms should be sliced and saved for topping.

2 Boil a pot of water for your noodles. In a separate saucepan, combine 1½ cups (360 ml) shio base, the stock, whipping cream, finely chopped mushrooms, bouillon cubes, and shichimi togarashi.

3 Bring to a boil, then lower the heat and let simmer until you are ready to serve. Right before serving, crank it back up to a boil.

4 Boil the noodles (if fresh, boil for about 1 minute; if packaged, boil for about 2 minutes). As soon as they're done, drain well and separate into serving bowls.

5 Pour 2 cups (480 ml) soup over each bowl of noodles. Top each bowl with the remaining mushrooms, cabbage, a dollop of fresh ginger, green onions, and an ajitsuke tamago.

CRISPY GREENS RAMEN

Level	2
Serves	6
Prep Time	30 minutes, plus time to make the base, noodles (optional), and toppings (optional)

I am a big fan of Swiss chard, kale, and brussels sprouts, but I love them even more when they are cooked crisp in the oven. They stay surprisingly crunchy in this ramen and really balance out the richness of the coconut milk.

To Make in Advance

Shio Base (page 20) or your base of choice

Ramen Noodles (page 24)

Poached Eggs (page 31)

Garlic Chips (page 39)

Ingredients

1 small bunch Swiss chard (I prefer rainbow chard), center vein removed and leaves chopped

1 small bunch kale (I prefer dino kale), center vein removed and leaves chopped

10 brussels sprouts, halved, thinly sliced

2 tbsp olive oil

Salt and black pepper

12 cups (1.8 L) vegetable or chicken stock

1½ cups (360 ml) coconut milk

3 tsp fish sauce

Additional Toppings

6 green onions, thinly sliced (1 tbsp per serving)

1 bunch cilantro, leaves only (small pile per serving)

1½ limes, quartered (1 quarter per serving)

1 Preheat the oven to 400°F (200°C). Put the rack in the middle position and line a baking sheet with parchment.

2 Wash and dry your Swiss chard and kale. Make sure there is no moisture left on the leaves. Chop the Swiss chard, kale, and brussels sprouts.

3 Toss your leaves with olive oil and sprinkle with salt and pepper. Place on the prepared baking sheet and bake for about 15 minutes, or until crisp. Watch carefully to avoid burning.

4 Boil a pot of water for your noodles. In a separate saucepan, combine 2¼ cups (540 ml) shio base, the stock, coconut milk, and fish sauce to a boil, then lower the heat and let simmer until it's ready to serve.

5 Boil the noodles (if fresh, boil for about 1 minute; if packaged, boil for about 2 minutes). As soon as they're done, drain well and separate into serving bowls.

6 Pour 2 cups (480 ml) soup over each bowl of noodles. Top with a mountain of crispy greens, green onions, cilantro, lime wedge, poached egg, and garlic chips.

⇥ CHEESE RAMEN ⇤

Level	3
Serves	4
Prep Time	30 minutes, plus time to make the bases, noodles (optional), and toppings (optional)

My friend Bradley, who often travels to Tokyo for business, insisted that I try his favorite cheese ramen shop, Tsukomo. They use a local artisan cheese called Golden Gouda that they grate paper-thin and then place in a huge mound on the ramen. The cheese melts into every bite. This is my rendition of that delicious creation. This recipe is all in the prep, so once you have your major components made ahead of time, you can throw it together quickly.

To Make in Advance

Tonkotsu Base (page 16)

Miso Base (page 14)

Ramen Noodles (page 24)

Ajitsuke Tamago (page 34)

Roasted Garlic Butter (page 38)

Ingredients

1 cup (100 g) brussels sprouts leaves

2 tbsp olive oil (I prefer smoked olive oil)

½ tsp kosher salt

1 cup (240 ml) chicken stock

1 cup (100 g) finely grated aged Gouda cheese (use a microplane to get it very fine)

Additional Topping

4 cups (400 g) finely grated aged Gouda cheese (1 cup, or 100 g, per serving)

1 Preheat the oven to 400°F (200°C). Put the rack in the middle position and line a baking sheet with parchment.

2 Toss the brussels sprouts leaves with olive oil and sprinkle with kosher salt. Arrange them in a single layer so that they do not touch and bake for about 10 minutes, or until crispy and brown around the edges. Watch carefully to avoid burning.

3 Boil a pot of water for your noodles. Take your whole roasted bulb of garlic (if using), remove the cloves, and smash them with the back of a knife to make a paste.

4 In a separate large saucepan, whisk 5 cups (1.1 L) tonkotsu base and ¼ cup (60 ml) miso base with the stock, roasted garlic paste, and grated Gouda until well combined. Bring to a boil, then lower the heat and let simmer until you are ready to serve. Right before serving, crank it back up to a boil.

5 Boil the noodles (if fresh, boil for about 1 minute; if packaged, boil for about 2 minutes). As soon as they're done, drain well and separate into serving bowls.

6 Pour 1½ cups (360 ml) cheesy soup over each bowl of noodles. Top each bowl with a big pile of cheese, a pile of crispy brussels sprouts, and an ajitsuke tamago.

VEGGIE RAINBOW RAMEN

Level	1
Serves	6
Prep Time	30 minutes, plus time to make the base, noodles (optional), and topping (optional)

I love how this dish appeals to all the senses. The beautiful colors, the smell of the soup, the crunch of the fresh menma, the velvety quality of the quail eggs, the delicate taste of the shoyu seasoning— it's veggie heaven and tastes as good as it looks.

To Make in Advance

Shoyu Base (page 18) or your base of choice

Ramen Noodles (page 24)

Menma (page 30)

Veggies

2 tbsp sesame oil

4 tbsp mirin (sweet rice wine)

2 garlic cloves, minced

2 tbsp grated ginger

6 tbsp shoyu (soy sauce)

1 red bell pepper, seeded and julienned

3 medium carrots, shredded

1 cup (50 g) bean sprouts

1 cup (75 g) snap peas

¼ head Napa cabbage, shredded

¼ head red cabbage, shredded

Additional Toppings

12 raw quail eggs (optional; 2 per serving)

4 tsp sesame seeds (I prefer black sesame seeds; ½ tsp per serving)

6 chives (I prefer garlic chives), chopped (small pile per serving)

1 Combine the sesame oil, mirin, garlic, ginger, and shoyu in a wok or medium skillet. Heat to high. Add the red pepper, carrots, bean sprouts, peas, and cabbage and cook for about 5 minutes, or until the cabbage wilts and the carrots are cooked through.

2 Boil a pot of water for your noodles. In a separate saucepan, bring 12 cups (2.8 L) shoyu base to a boil, then lower the heat and let simmer until you are ready to serve. Right before serving, crank it back up to a boil.

3 Boil the noodles (if fresh, boil for about 1 minute; if packaged, boil for about 2 minutes). As soon as they're done, drain well and separate into serving bowls.

4 Pour 2 cups (480 ml) soup over each bowl of noodles. Top with the vegetable mixture, menma, and quail eggs. Garnish with the sesame seeds and chives.

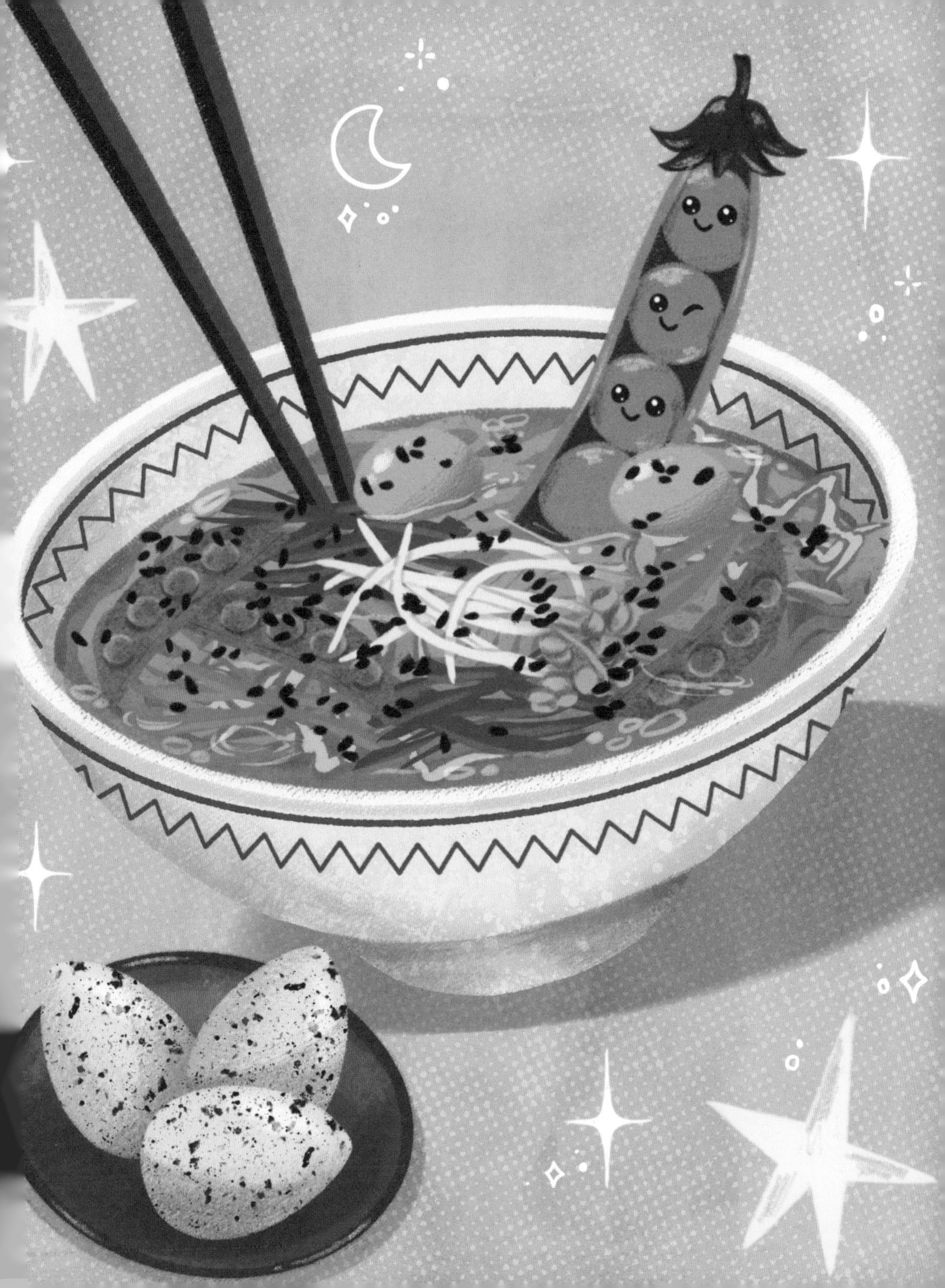

SPICY & COLD RAMEN

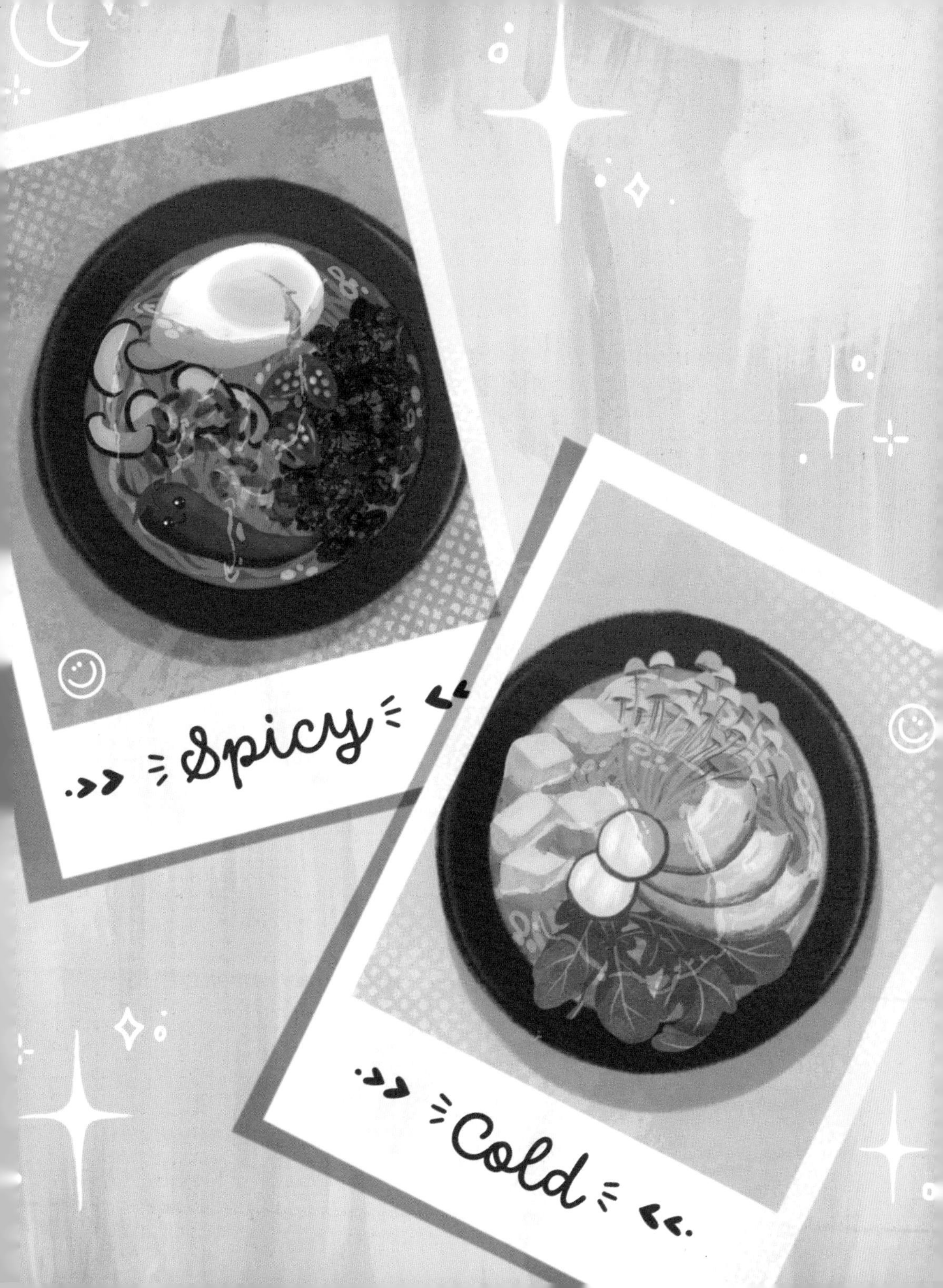
Spicy
Cold

⇥ CHORIZO MISO RAMEN ⇤

Level ⬤ 2

Serves ⬤ 6

Prep Time   45 minutes, plus time to make the base, noodles (optional), and topping (optional)

The inspiration for this chorizo-infused miso base came to me when I was standing in line with my sister Kathleen at La Super Rica Taqueria, the Santa Barbara taco stand made famous by Juila Child. I was excited to discover how well the chorizo blended into the soup base. The result is a vibrant, full-flavor Mexican take on ramen.

To Make in Advance

Miso Base (page 14) or your base of choice

Ramen Noodles (page 24)

Poached Eggs (page 31)

Ingredients

½ red onion, peeled

2 red bell peppers, seeded

2 green chilies, seeded

1 tbsp vegetable oil

3 ears sweet white corn (½ ear per serving)

1 lb (455 g) chorizo, casings removed

12 cups (2.8 L) chicken or vegetable stock

Additional Toppings

1 bunch kale (small pile per serving)

1 bunch radishes, thinly sliced (3 slices per serving)

1 Add the onion, peppers, and chilies to a food processor and pulse until finely chopped.

2 Heat the oil in a large skillet over medium-high heat. Add the onion-peppers mixture, cook for 10 minutes, and transfer to a bowl.

3 Steam the corn, let cool a bit, and then remove the kernels from the ears.

4 To the same skillet you used for the onion-peppers mixture above, add the chorizo and cook, breaking it into small pieces with a wooden spoon, until it is browned.

5 Boil a pot of water for your noodles. In a separate saucepan, bring 2¼ cups (540 ml) miso base and the stock to a boil. Add 6 tablespoons of cooked chorizo to your soup, then lower the heat and let simmer until you are ready to serve. *Note: It's 3 tablespoons base to 1 cup (240 ml) stock. Right before serving, crank it back up to a boil.*

6 Boil the noodles (if fresh, boil for about 1 minute; if packaged, boil for about 2 minutes). As soon as they're done, drain well and separate into serving bowls.

7 Pour 2 cups (480 ml) soup over each bowl of noodles. Top each bowl with a small mound of corn and chorizo, kale, ¼ cup (40 g) of the onion-peppers mixture, radishes, and a poached egg.

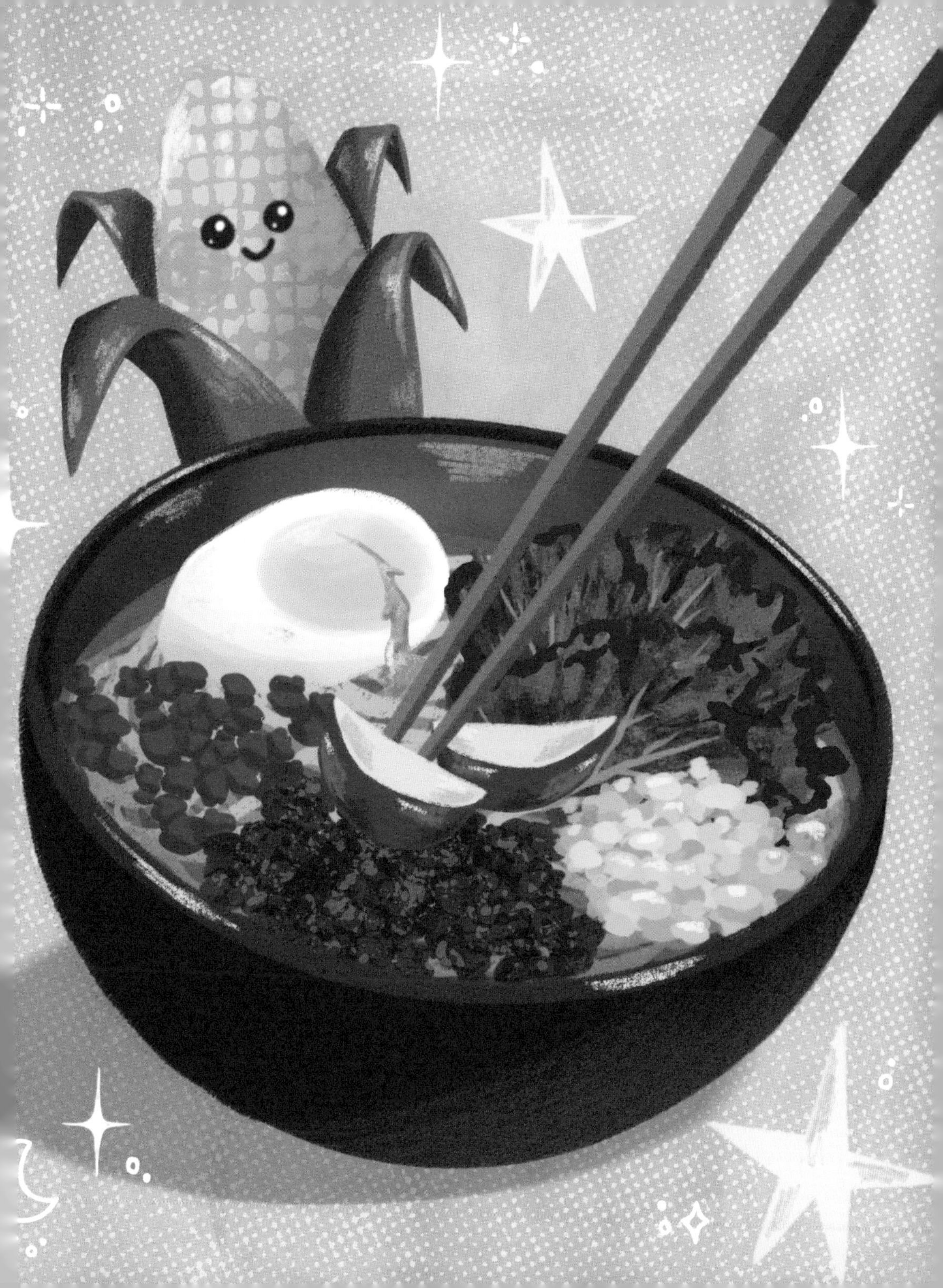

→ SPICY PORK TANTANMEN ←

Level	2
Serves	6
Prep Time	30 minutes, plus time to make the noodles (optional)

On my ramen tour of Tokyo, I was taken to LaShowHan for *tantanmen*, which translates to "red hot chili noodle," and the dish is a Japanese adaptation of a Szechuan-style spicy noodle dish known as Dan Dan noodles. The owner's, Kenichi Okada, tantanmen is the inspiration for this recipe.

To Make in Advance

Ramen Noodles (page 24)

Ingredients

1 red bell pepper

2 tbsp sesame oil

1 lb (455 g) ground pork

2 tsp chili oil

1 tsp salt

1 tbsp sugar

1 tbsp shoyu (soy sauce)

2 tbsp chili paste

¼ cup (60 g) sesame paste or tahini

⅛ tsp ground Szchuan peppercorns (substitute Tasmanian pepper)

3 cups (720 ml) chicken stock

Additional Toppings

6 green onions, thinly sliced (1 tbsp per serving)

6 tbsp unsalted peanuts, crushed (1 tbsp per serving)

1 bunch daikon radish sprouts (substitute alfalfa sprouts; small pile per serving)

Sesame oil

3 tsp chili paste (½ tsp per serving)

1 Heat the whole pepper over an open flame on a gas stove or grill until all sides are completely black and charred. Remove the skin from the pepper and slice open, removing the stem and seeds.

2 Add the pepper to a food processor or blender and process until smooth.

3 Heat the sesame oil in a wok or large skillet over medium-high heat. Add the ground pork and cook until no longer pink, breaking it up with a wooden spoon. Remove the pork and pulse in a food processor until a fine mince.

4 Warm the chili oil in the wok over medium-high heat and add the minced pork. Stir in the red pepper puree, salt, sugar, shoyu, chili paste, sesame paste, and ground peppercorns and fry until all the aromatics combine.

5 Boil a pot of water for your noodles. Add the stock to the wok, bring to a boil, then lower to a simmer for 10 minutes to absorb all the spices. Stock should evaporate a little and the sauce will be thick.

6 Boil the noodles (if fresh, boil for about 1 minute; if packaged, boil for about 2 minutes). As soon as they're done, drain well.

7 Pour ¾ cup (180 ml) sauce into each serving bowl, top with noodles, and garnsih with the green onions, peanuts, daikon radish sprouts, a drizzle of sesame oil, and chili paste.

→ SPICY TOFU RAMEN ←

Level 2

Serves 6

Prep Time 20 minutes, plus time to make the soup bases, noodles (optional), and toppings (optional)

This recipe incorporates the Spicy Base with five other To Make in Advance recipes that can all be prepared ahead of time. I know it seems daunting to think about pulling this together, but the only recipe that really needs to be done the day you plan to eat it is the Agedashi-Doufu. Everything else can be done days before so that it takes less than thirty minutes to get this to the table.

To Make in Advance
Miso Base (page 14) or your base of choice
Spicy Base (page 22)
Ramen Noodles (page 24)
Agedashi-Doufu (page 100)
Menma (page 30)
Roasted Nori (page 33)

Ingredient
12 cups (1.8 L) chicken or vegetable stock

Additional Toppings
1 large package aburaage tofu (½ pocket per serving)
1 bunch mizuna lettuce (substitute arugula; small pile per serving)
2 raw quail eggs (optional)

1 If using, cut the roasted nori into small strips with kitchen scissors.

2 On an ungreased baking sheet, broil the aburaage tofu for about 2 minutes, or until it crisps up. Julienne it into small strips.

3 Prepare the agedashi-doufu according to the recipe without the sauce accompaniment.

4 Boil a pot of water for your noodles. In a separate saucepan, combine 2¼ cups (540 ml) miso base, the stock, and 3 cups (720 ml) spicy base to a boil, then lower the heat and let simmer until it's ready to serve. *Note: It's 3 tablespoons base to 1 cup (240 ml) stock. Right before serving, crank it back up to a boil.*

5 Boil the noodles (if fresh, boil for about 1 minute; if packaged, boil for about 2 minutes). As soon as they're done, drain well and separate into serving bowls.

6 Pour 2 cups (480 ml) soup over each bowl of noodles. Top each bowl with a couple squares of agedashi-doufu, a pile of aburaage tofu strips, a small pile of arugula, a portion of menma, and 2 quail eggs (if using). Finish with a sprinkling of roasted nori strips.

HIYASHI CHUKA RAMEN

Level: 1

Serves: 6

Prep Time: 20 minutes, plus time to make the broth, noodles (optional), and toppings (optional)

***Hiyashi chuka* means "chilled Chinese" ramen, but as with many Chinese dishes, the Japanese have made their own version. This refreshing ramen-type salad with cold broth is normally served in the summer, with its colors speaking to what's in season. There are all kinds of variations of this, so feel free to substitute with what you have fresh on hand for your own version.**

To Make in Advance

Cold Noodle Broth (page 23)

Ramen Noodles (page 24)

Chashu (page 32)

Beni Shoga (page 33)

Eggs

2 eggs

¼ tsp salt

½ tsp sugar

1 tsp vegetable oil

Additional toppings

6 slices (170 g) Black Forest ham, julienned (1 slice, or 28 g, per serving)

2 cups (100 g) bean sprouts (⅓ cup, or 17 g, per serving)

1 Japanese cucumber, seeded and julienned (¼ cup, or 25 g, per serving)

3 medium carrots, shredded (½ carrot per serving)

3 sheets nori, julienned (½ sheet per serving)

Roasted sesame seeds

1 Boil a pot of water for your noodles. Boil the noodles (if fresh, boil for about 1 minute; if packaged, boil for about 2 minutes). As soon as they're done, drain well and refrigerate in a bath of cold water for at least 1 hour.

2 Beat the eggs with the salt and sugar.

3 Heat the vegetable oil in a large skillet over medium heat. Pour the egg mixture into a pan and make a very thin omelet, like a crepe. Remove with a spatula and let cool. Roll up like a cigar and shred thinly with a knife.

4 Drain the cold noodles well and separate into serving bowls. Pour 1 cup (240 ml) cold noodle broth over each bowl of chilled noodles. Top each bowl with eggs, ham, bean sprouts, cucumber, carrots, chashu, and a small amount of beni shoga. Garnish with roasted nori strips and sesame seeds.

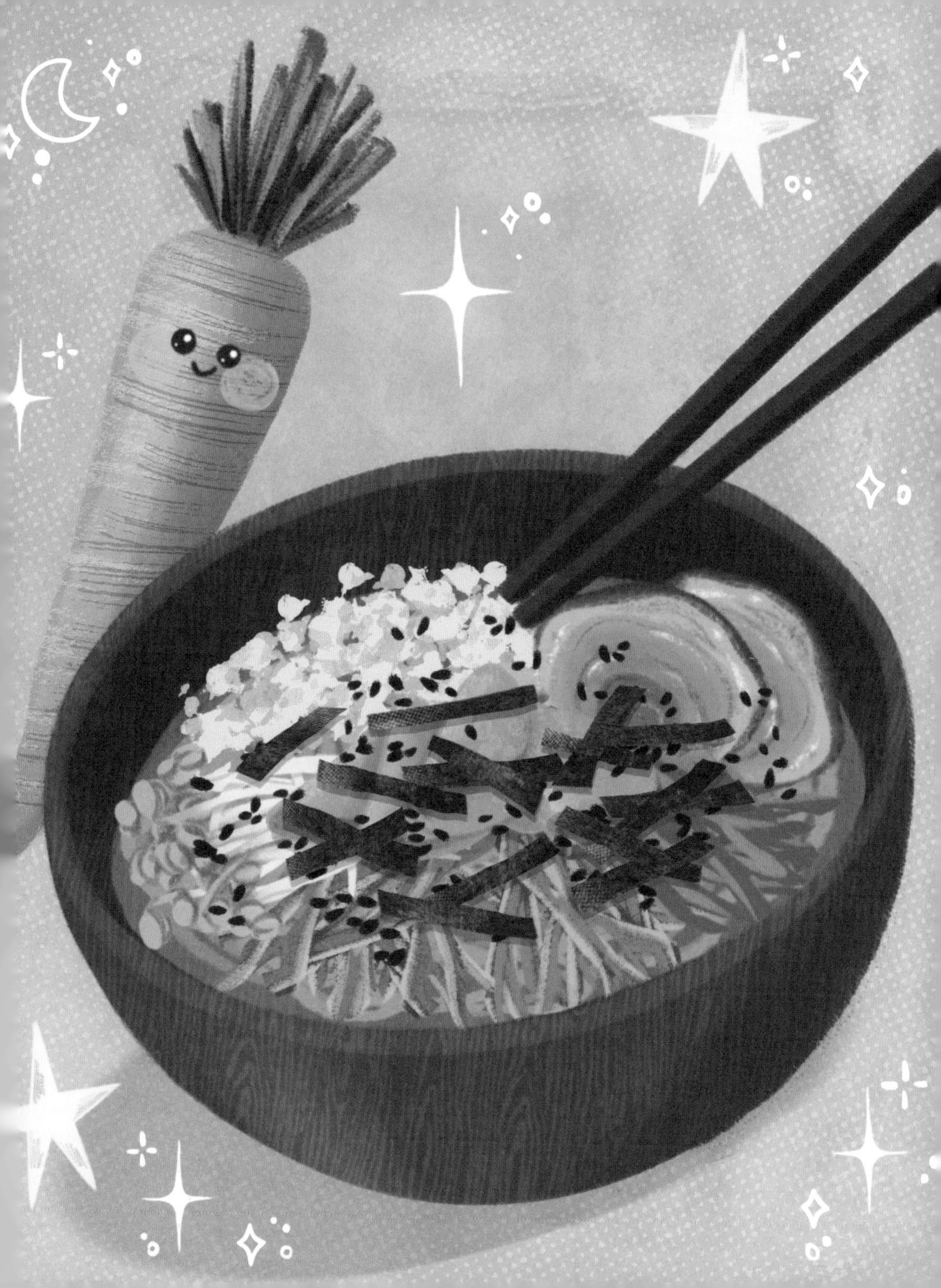

⇒ MAPO TOFU RAMEN ⇐

Level	3
Serves	4
Prep Time	1 hour, plus time to make base, noodles (optional), and topping (optional)

This is another great recipe that my friend Emily Lai helped me to develop. We are lucky to have her food background and expertise in helping make this delicious rendition of mapo tofu, full of spice and flavor. The Tonkotsu Base gives it the perfect thickness, and the spice level is just right.

To Make in Advance

Tonkotsu Base (page 16)

Ramen Noodles (page 24)

Poached Eggs (page 31)

Ingredients

4 tbsp cornstarch

4 tbsp water

1 tbsp vegetable oil

2 garlic cloves, minced

1 shallot, minced

½ lb (225 g) ground pork

1 tsp salt

4 oz (115 g) shiitake mushrooms, sliced, divided

1 tbsp chili sauce (I prefer Sambal Oelek)

4 tbsp Shaoxing wine, divided (substitute dry sherry)

1 block medium-firm tofu, cubed

1 tbsp sesame oil

1 tbsp chili oil

Additional Toppings

4 green onions, thinly sliced (1 tbsp per serving)

1 bunch daikon radish sprouts (substitute alfalfa sprouts; small pile per serving)

1 tsp shichimi togarashi, optional (1 pinch per serving)

1 In a small bowl, whisk the cornstarch and water to make a slurry.

2 Heat the vegetable oil in a medium skillet over medium-high heat, add the garlic and shallot and sweat them for about 30 seconds. Add the pork and break it up into small pieces. Sprinkle with salt. Add half of the shiitake mushrooms and continue to stir until pork is fully cooked. Stir in the chili sauce. Pour in half the dry sherry to deglaze the pan, stirring to pick up any bits from the bottom of the pan.

3 Heat 8 cups (1.8 L) of tonkotsu base in a large pot. Add the pork mixture and tofu and let simmer for 10 minutes.

4 Heat the sesame oil in a medium saucepan over medium-high heat. Add the remaining shiitake mushrooms, sprinkle with salt and sauté for 3 to 4 minutes. Deglaze with the remaining dry sherry.

5 Boil a pot of water for your noodles. Crank up the heat your tonkotsu base and add the chili oil and the cornstarch slurry to thicken. Keep at a boil until ready to serve.

6 Boil the noodles (if fresh, boil for about 1 minute; if packaged, boil for about 2 minutes). As soon as they're done, drain well and separate into serving bowls.

7 Pour 2 cups (480 ml) soup over each bowl of noodles. Top each bowl with the green onions, daikon radish sprouts, sautéed mushrooms, and a poached egg and sprinkle with shichimi togarashi.

⇒ CHILLED CUCUMBER TSUKEMEN ⇐

Level **1**

Serves **4**

Prep Time 20 minutes, plus time to make the broth, noodles (optional), and topping (optional)

Tsukemen **refers to a dish of noodles that are served separately and dipped in a flavorful soup that coats the noodles and seasons every bite. It's not usually chilled, so this is my own version.**

To Make in Advance

Cold Noodle Broth (page 23)

Ramen Noodles (page 24)

Kakuni (page 36)

Cucumber Soup

2 lbs (900 g) cucumbers (2 or 3 cucumbers), peeled, seeded, and chopped

2 yellow bell peppers, seeded and chopped

2 green onions, chopped

1 tbsp mint leaves

½ tsp grated ginger

1 tsp salt

¼ tsp white pepper

Additional Topping

1 cucumber, julienned (small bunch per serving)

1 Boil a pot of water for your noodles. Boil the noodles (if fresh, boil for about 1 minute; if packaged, boil for about 2 minutes). As soon as they're done, drain well and refrigerate in a bath of cold water for at least 1 hour.

2 Add the cucumbers, peppers, green onions, mint, and ginger to a blender with 2 cups (480 ml) of the cold noodle broth. Blend until very smooth and frothy. Transfer the soup to the refrigerator and chill for at least 2 hours.

3 After the soup has chilled, season it with salt and white pepper.

4 Drain the cold noodles well and separate into serving bowls. Serve the chilled noodles with 1 cup (240 ml) of the cold soup per serving in separate bowls. The noodles are for dipping into the cold soup. Top the noodles with the julienned cucumber and sliced kakuni.

→ SLOW-ROASTED TOMATO AND MISO SPINACH CHILLED RAMEN ←

Level	2
Serves	6
Prep Time	2½ hours, plus time to make the broth, noodles (optional), and topping

The tender and herb-laden slow-roasted tomatoes really are the star of this dish. The spinach is reminiscent of traditional Japanese *goma-ae*, made by coating spinach with sesame paste.

To Make in Advance

Cold Noodle Broth (page 23)

Ramen Noodles (page 24)

Poached Eggs (page 31)

Roasted Tomatoes

½ cup (120 ml) olive oil

2 sprigs fresh rosemary, chopped

2 sprigs thyme, chopped

1 tsp salt

⅛ tsp white pepper

2½ lbs (1.1 kg) tomatoes, stems removed and halved horizontally

Miso Spinach

3 tsp sesame oil, divided

1 lb (455 g) baby spinach leaves, washed and dried

1 tbsp sesame paste or tahini

2 tbsp shoyu (soy sauce)

2 tbsp mirin (sweet rice wine)

Additional toppings

2 cups (100 g) bean sprouts (⅓ cup, or 17 g, per serving)

Roasted sesame seeds

1 Preheat the oven to 325ºF (170ºC) with the rack set in the middle position. Combine the olive oil, rosemary, thyme, salt, and pepper in a shallow baking pan. Add the tomatoes and toss until well coated, laying them cut sides down before cooking. Roast for 2 hours, or until they are completely wilted and soft.

2 Meanwhile, boil a pot of water for your noodles. Boil the noodles (if fresh, boil for about 1 minute; if packaged, boil for about 2 minutes). As soon as they're done, drain well and refrigerate in a bath of cold water for at least 1 hour.

3 Cook the spinach in 3 batches. Heat 1 teaspoon sesame oil in a large skillet over medium-high heat. Add the spinach leaves and sauté, moving around frequently, until just cooked, about 1 minute. Remove and set in a bowl. Repeat with additional batches. When the spinach cools, squeeze out any excess water.

4 In a small bowl, whisk together the sesame paste, shoyu, and mirin until combined. Add the spinach and coat with the sauce.

5 Drain the cold noodles well and separate into serving bowls. Pour 2 cups (480 ml) cold noodle broth over each bowl of chilled noodles. Top each bowl with two roasted tomatoes, spinach, a mound of bean sprouts, and a poached egg. Garnish with roasted sesame seeds.

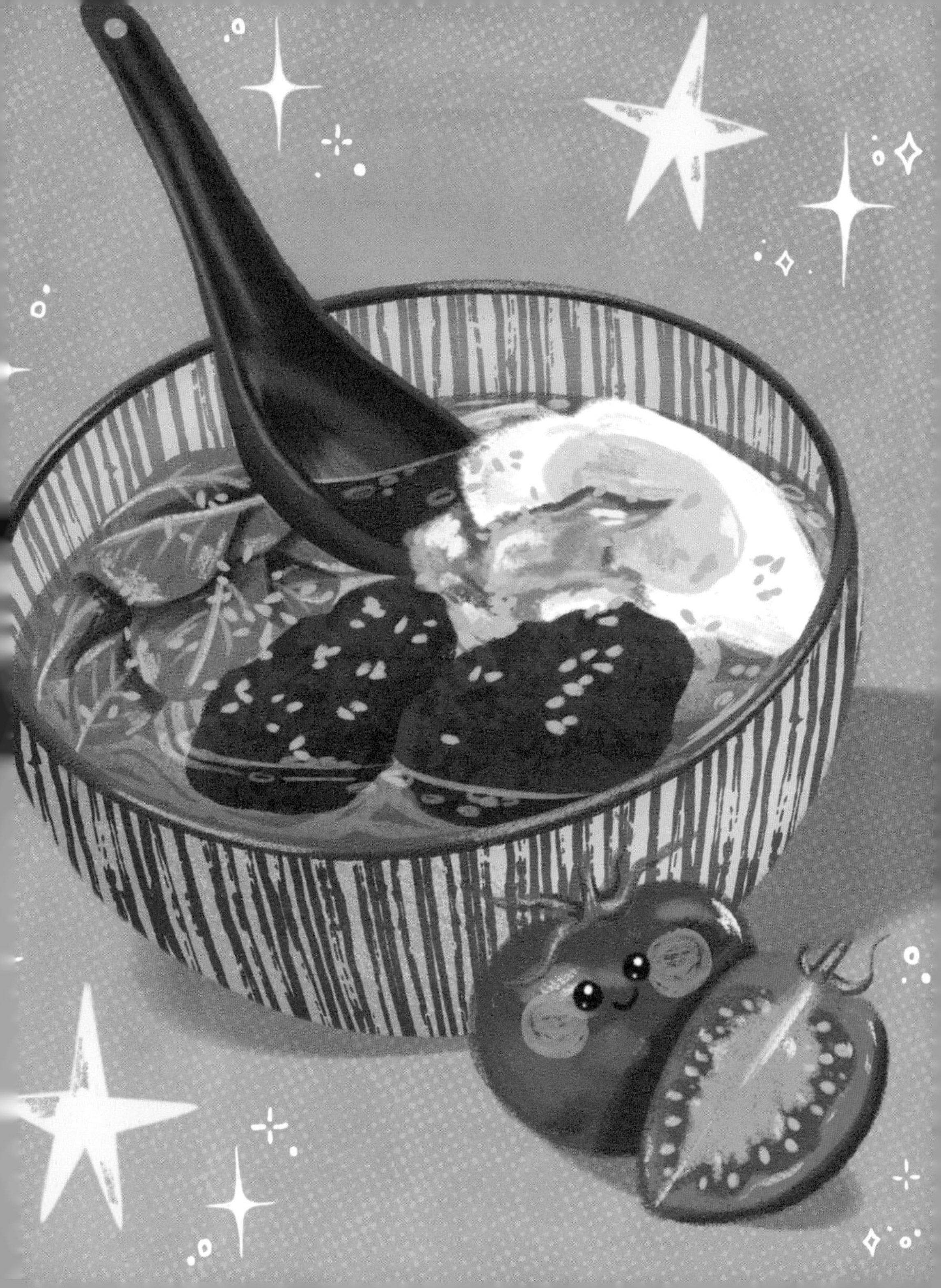

SIDES

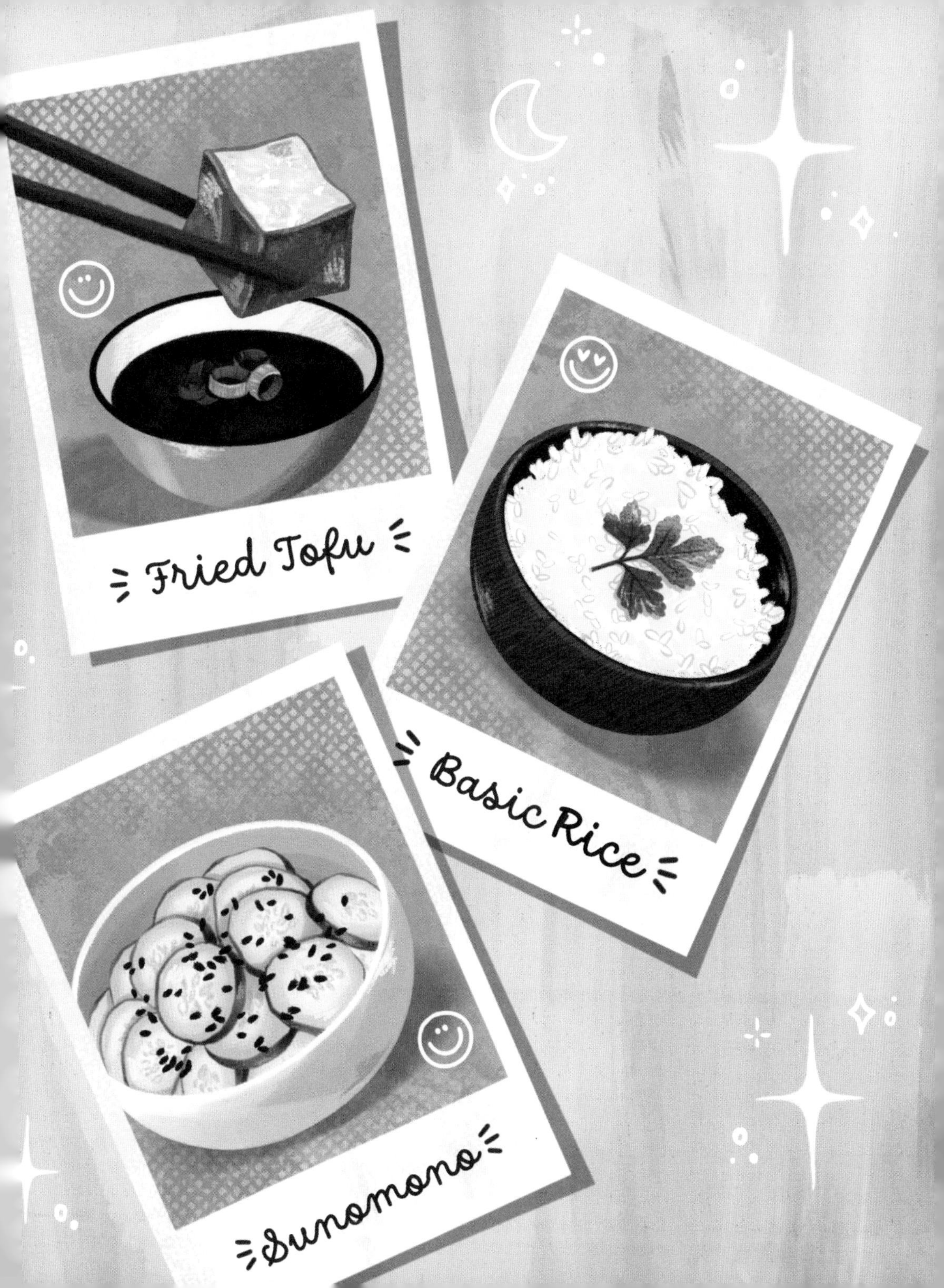
Fried Tofu
Basic Rice
Sunomono

→ AGEDASHI-DOUFU (FRIED TOFU) ←

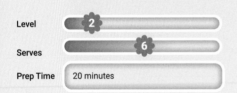

Level	2
Serves	6
Prep Time	20 minutes

When I ordered this in a restaurant, I couldn't understand how the tofu could stay crispy when it's swimming in sauce. I found out the trick here is to just lightly dust the tofu before frying it to achieve a delicate crispiness and still maintain a smooth and silky center. Too much batter makes it gummy.
A daikon grater is essential here; try one and you'll see what a difference it makes.

Fried Tofu

2 blocks soft tofu

Vegetable oil, for frying

3 tbsp cornstarch (I prefer katakuriko, or Japanese potato starch)

Sauce

1 packet dashi granules (keep in packet form)

2 cups (480 ml) water

3 tbsp shoyu (soy sauce)

2 tsp mirin (sweet rice wine)

2 tbsp sake

Garnish

1 daikon, peeled and grated with excess liquid squeezed out

4 or 5 chives (I prefer garlic chives), chopped

Bonito fish flakes, optional (1 tsp per serving)

1 To make the fried tofu: Drain the tofu and wrap it carefully in a paper towel. Set it on a plate in the refrigerator for 20 minutes to get all the moisture out. Remove, unwrap, and cut the tofu into cubes 1 inch (2.5 cm) wide.

2 To make the sauce: In a small saucepan, combine the dashi packet, water, shoyu, mirin, and sake. Bring to a boil, then lower to a simmer and cover. Let simmer for 10 minutes. Remove the dashi packet and keep covered on a low simmer until ready to use.

3 In a large deep skillet, add enough oil so that the tofu can be completely submerged (about 1½ inches, or 4 cm). Heat over high to approximately 375ºF (190ºC), or when a small piece of the tofu sizzles immediately when added.

4 While the oil is heating, lightly dust the cornstarch onto the tofu so that it is completely covered on all sides. You can use a sieve to dust or make a little duster out of cheesecloth tied with baking string. With a slotted spoon, gently lay the pieces of tofu in the hot oil, being careful not to overcrowd them. Cook in batches while rolling each piece over to cook on all sides. Remove when the tofu barely changes color and becomes crisp and almost inflated-looking. Do not brown. Transfer to a paper towel to drain.

5 Arrange a couple spoonfuls of the sauce in a serving dish and lay a couple pieces of tofu in the sauce. Garnish with the daikon, chives, and bonito fish flakes, if you like.

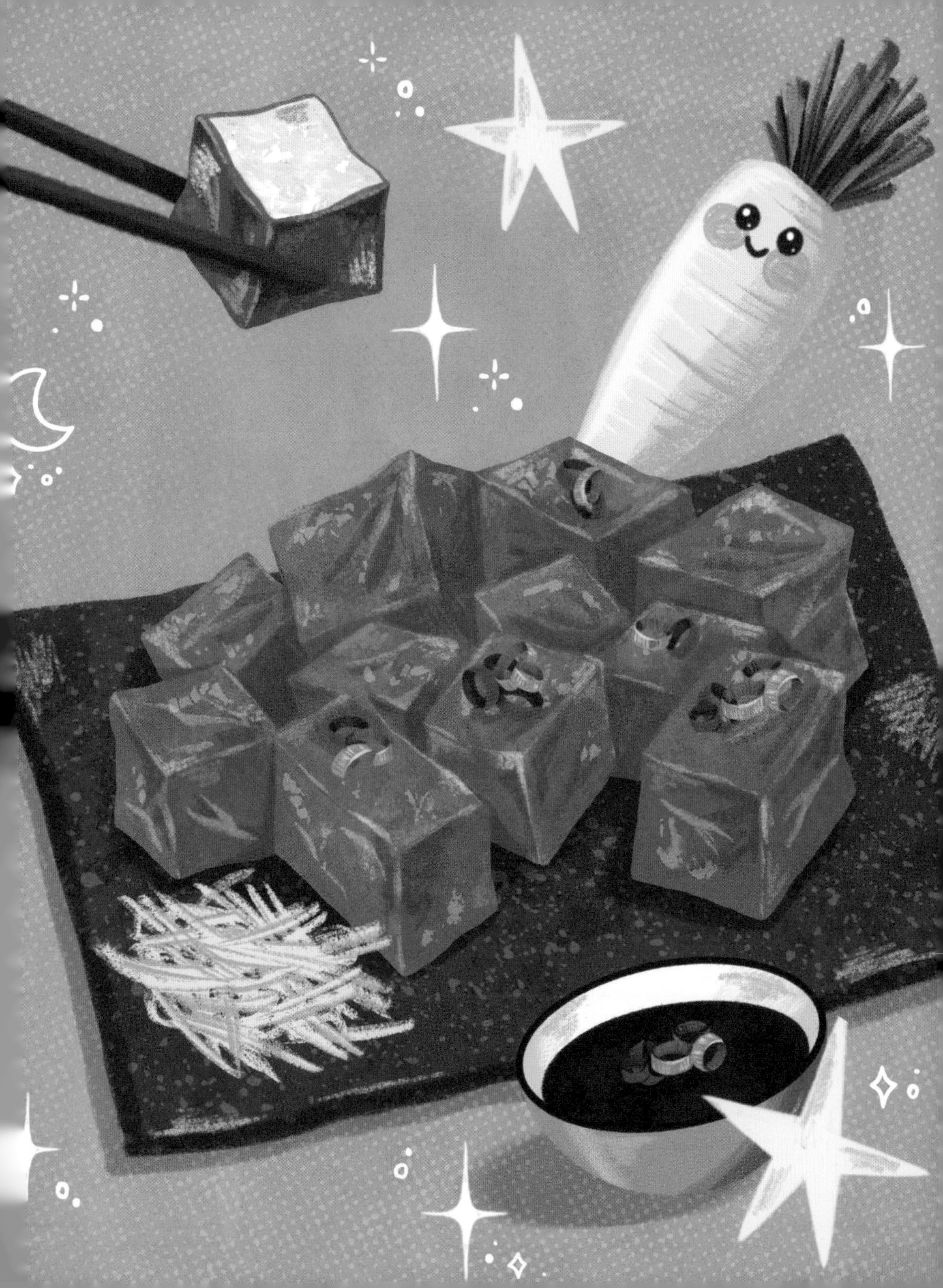

⇥ BASIC JAPANESE RICE ⇤

Level	1
Makes	As much as you need
Prep Time	25 minutes

Japanese rice is shorter grained and higher in starch content than other rice, which gives it its stickier consistency. The rice needs to be washed multiple times to rinse off the surface starch and hydrate the grains. I actually prefer short-grain brown rice, which is cooked in the same manner. When you've had an excellent bowl of rice, you'll know. If you don't have a rice cooker, follow these easy instructions for the stovetop.

Ingredients

2 cups (400 g) Japanese short-grain white rice*
1 qt or 4 cups (1 L) water

If you want to increase the amount of rice, add 2 cups (480 ml) additional water for every 1 cup (200 g) rice.

1 In a medium saucepan, add the rice and thoroughly rinse it in the sink by pouring water over the rice until it is covered by about 2 inches (5 cm) of water. Swirl and squeeze the rice and water with your hands until the water looks milky. Carefully pour out the milky water, leaving the rice. Repeat three times, or until the water runs clear. Once the water runs clear, give it a final drain.

2 Cover the rice with 1 quart or 4 cups (1 L) water to begin cooking. Place the lid on the pan and start cooking the rice over high heat until the water comes to a boil. Lower the heat to just above a simmer and cook for 20 minutes (brown rice may require more cooking time). Do not remove the lid when cooking as steam will be released, extending the cooking time.

3 Remove from the heat and let steam with the lid on for an additional 10 minutes before serving.

CHAHAN FRIED RICE

Level 1

Serves 8

Prep Time 20 minutes, plus time to make the rice

In Japan, you'll often see fried rice offered on the menu at ramen shops alongside fried dumplings. In my home growing up, we ate fried rice for breakfast. My own recipe has changed over the years, but this is a basic one that you can add almost anything to. The options are endless, so feel free to experiment.

To Make in Advance
Basic Japanese Rice (page 102)

Ingredients
4 slices bacon

¼ red onion, finely chopped

1 tbsp sesame oil

4 cups (745 g) cooked Basic Japanese Rice

2 eggs

2 tbsp shoyu (soy sauce)

1 tsp sriracha (optional)

1 In a medium or large skillet, cook the bacon over medium-high heat until well done. Set aside on a paper towel and crumble when cooled. Do not discard your bacon grease.

2 In the pan with leftover bacon grease, sauté the onions over medium-high heat until they start to brown, stirring frequently, about 2 minutes.

3 Add the sesame oil to the onions. Immediately add the rice and incorporate until it is coated with the grease, oil, and onions. The rice will start to make a popping sound as it gets crispy. Make a well in the middle of the rice and crack the eggs into it. Take a fork or chopsticks and mix the eggs in the middle. Combine the egg and rice until the eggs cook through; you'll be able to see little pieces of cooked egg throughout as it completely cooks.

4 Add the shoyu and Sriracha (if using) and mix through.

5 Mix in the crumbled bacon right before serving to preserve its crispiness and serve warm.

⇝ AUNTIE BETTY'S SHRIMP GYOZA ⇜

Level	2
Makes	30
Prep Time	1 hour

My Auntie Betty is a legendary cook in our family. She gets a special Dace fish paste from May Wah supermarket in the Richmond District of San Francisco. My auntie's inspiration came from a little restaurant in San Francisco that used to make the most delicious gyoza. The owner gave her the recipe without any real measurements, but through trial and error, she perfected it.

Shrimp Gyoza

30 raw shrimp, peeled, deveined, and cleaned

½ cup (125 g) fish paste (I prefer Dace fish paste)

¼ cup (62.5 g) dried dill

1 large garlic clove, minced

1 tbsp unsalted butter, melted

2 tbsp heavy cream

1 tsp white pepper

1 package round wonton wrappers

4 tbsp vegetable oil

⅛ cup (30 ml) chicken stock

Dipping Sauce

½ cup (120 ml) shoyu (soy sauce)

¼ cup (60 ml) white vinegar

5 drops chili oil

1 To make the shrimp gyoza: Cut each shrimp into three or four ½-inch (6 mm) pieces.

2 Combine the shrimp, fish paste, dill, garlic, butter, cream, and pepper in a medium bowl. Drop a spoonful of the shrimp mixture onto each wonton wrapper. Fold over and use hot water with your finger around half the round and fold over to seal.

3 Line a baking sheet with aluminum foil and lay the wontons in a row; it's fine if they touch each other. If you want to serve them at a later date, freeze on an unlined baking sheet overnight, then transfer to a sealed bag to store.

4 To make the sauce: In a small bowl, whisk together all the sauce ingredients until combined.

5 Heat the vegetable oil in a large skillet over medium-high heat. Add the gyoza and cook until browned on both sides. Do not crowd the pan. Pour the stock into the pan, cover, and let simmer for 4 minutes. Remove and serve with the sauce.

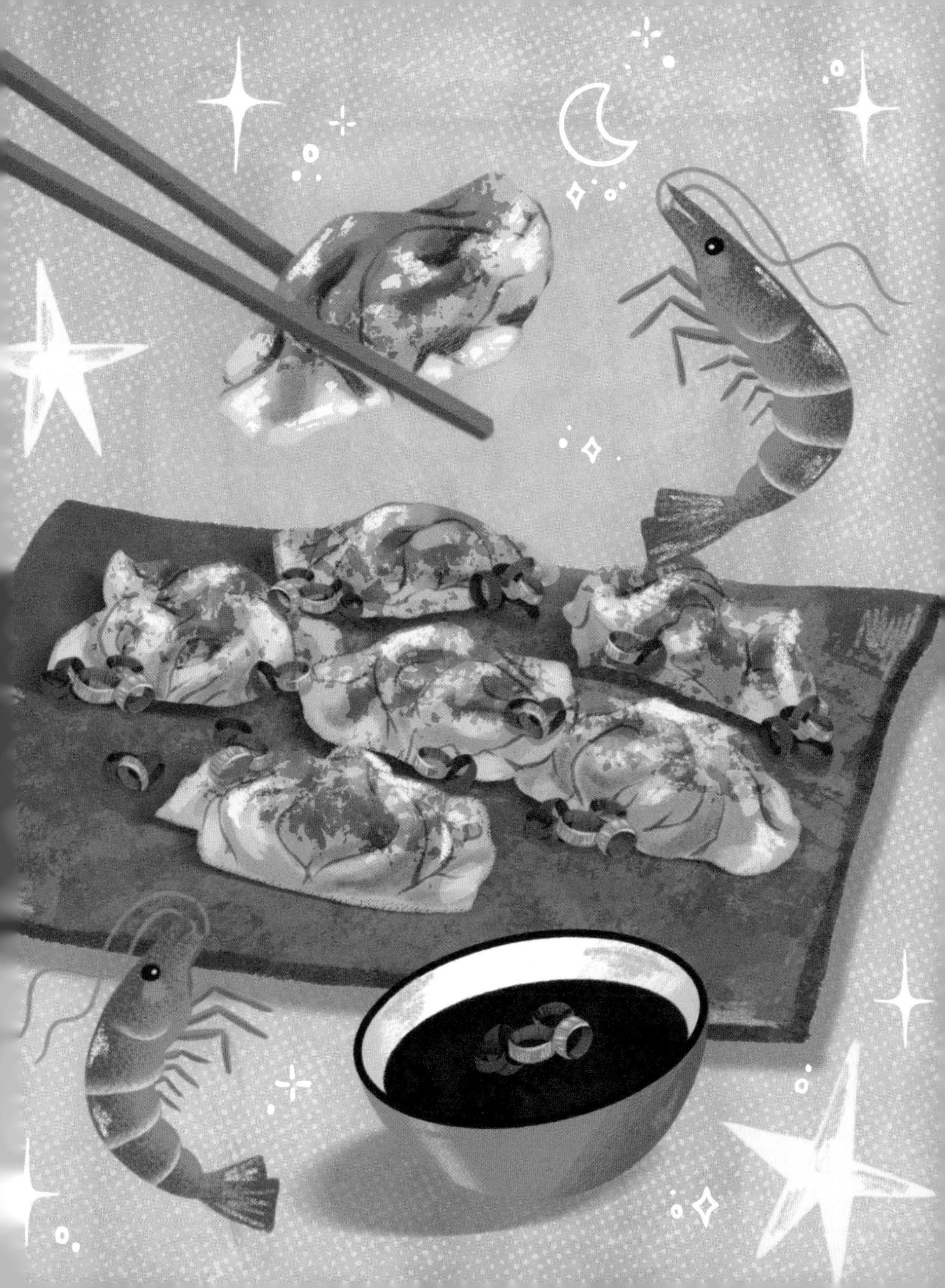

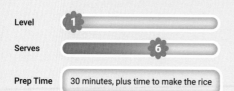

SWEET PORK GOHAN (RICE)

Level	1
Serves	6
Prep Time	30 minutes, plus time to make the rice

This recipe was inspired by my blogger friend Brian of *Ramen Adventures*. He had just returned from Hiroshima, where they were in the midst of a soupless tantanmen (Japanese version of a spicy Chinese-style ramen; see Spicy Pork Tantanmen on page 90) boom. When you finish the noodles, there is a sludge of tare, ground pork, and green onions left in the bowl, to which you are meant to add rice. This is a very simplified, non-spicy variation.

To Make in Advance

Basic Japanese Rice (page 102)

Ingredients

½ onion

1 carrot, peeled and cut into thirds

1 tbsp sesame oil

1 lb (455 g) ground pork

2 tbsp shoyu (soy sauce)

2 tbsp sugar

1 tbsp sake

1 tsp grated ginger

6 cups (1.1 kg) cooked Basic Japanese Rice

3 green onions, thinly sliced, for garnish

1 Pulse the onion and carrot in a food processor until finely chopped, or chop finely by hand.

2 Heat the sesame oil in a large skillet over medium-high heat. Add the onion-carrot mixture and sauté until the onions are translucent, about 10 minutes. Add the ground pork and cook until no longer pink. Lower the heat to a simmer.

3 In a small bowl, whisk together the shoyu, sugar, sake, and ginger until well combined. Pour the sauce over the pork and stir to incorporate.

4 Transfer the pork mixture to food processor and process until a fine consistency. (Alternatively, you can use an immersion blender in the pan to pulse.)

5 To serve, prepare a bowl of warm rice and ladle a generous portion of the sweet pork over the top. Garnish with the chopped green onions.

⇒ CUCUMBER SUNOMONO (SALAD) ⇐

Level	3
Serves	6
Prep Time	20 minutes, plus 1 hour chilling

This light and refreshing salad is the perfect accompaniment to a rich and filling bowl of ramen. The trick to making the cucumbers soak up all the delicious dressing is to cut them wafer-thin with a mandoline.

Ingredients

2 cucumbers (I prefer Japanese or English cucumbers)

¼ tsp salt, plus more for sprinkling

1 tsp dried wakame (optional)

½ cup (100 g) sugar

½ cup (120 ml) Japanese rice vinegar

1 tsp shoyu (soy sauce)

Toppings (optional)

Freshly cracked crab

Cooked baby shrimp

Chopped octopus

1 Slice the cucumber with a mandoline on the lowest setting for a very thin cut. Place in a bowl and sprinkle with salt, stir to incorporate, and set aside. This will help get all the water out of the cucumber slices so that the salad is not soggy.

2 Soak the wakame in water for about 10 minutes. Squeeze out all excess water and julienne into thin strips. Whisk together the sugar, vinegar, ¼ teaspoon salt, and shoyu. Add the wakame.

3 Transfer the salted cucumbers to a colander and rinse with cold water. Squeeze out the excess water from the cucumbers and add to the vinegar mixture.

4 Chill for at least 1 hour before serving. If desired, top with crab, shrimp, or octopus.

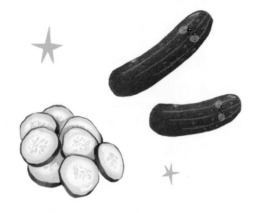

⇒ COUSIN JILLY'S PAN CHIRASHIZUSHI DYNAMITE ⇐

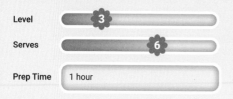

Level **3**

Serves **6**

Prep Time 1 hour

Chirashizushi, or scattered sushi, is traditionally made by scattering raw fish and vegetables over sushi rice. This variation made by my cousin Jill mixes the ingredients into the rice and is topped with a crab dynamite mixture, like those found on top of sushi, that bakes up golden brown and is simply delicious.

Ingredients

3 cups (585 g) uncooked Japanese short-grain white rice

1 large rectangular piece kombu (about 10 inches, or 25 cm, long), cut into large squares

3¼ cups (780 ml) water

⅓ cup (80 ml) rice wine vinegar

⅓ cup (65 g) plus 1 tbsp sugar, divided

1 tsp salt

2 eggs

2 tbsp vegetable oil, divided

2 tbsp shoyu (soy sauce)

½ lotus root, peeled, halved, and finely sliced

2 medium carrots, peeled and shredded

¼ cup (26 g) Nori Komi Furikake (available at most Asian markets or online)

5 shiitake mushrooms, cut into ¼-inch (6 mm) dice

½ onion, diced

1 cup (135 g) cooked crab meat

¾ cup (175 g) mayonnaise

¾ cup (175 g) sour cream

Cucumber Sunomono (page 107), to serve (optional)

Roasted Nori (page 33), to serve (optional)

1 Preheat the oven to 350°F (180°C) with the rack in the middle position.

2 In a large pot or a rice cooker, rinse and drain the rice to remove impurities. Do this three or four times, or until the water runs clear. Add the kombu and cover with the 3¼ cups (780 ml) water. Let soak for 30 minutes. If you have a rice cooker, transfer the rice to it and follow the instructions. If you don't, cook your pot over high heat with the lid on. After the water has been boiling for 30 seconds, lower the heat to a simmer and continue cooking for 14 to 15 minutes. Briefly turn up the heat again, then remove from heat. Keeping the lid on, let the rice to steam for about 10 minutes.

3 In a small saucepan, whisk the vinegar, ⅓ cup (65 g) of the sugar, and salt. Bring to a boil, stirring often until the sugar dissolves. Remove from the heat.

4 In a small bowl, whisk the eggs. Heat 1 tablespoon of the vegetable oil in a saucepan over medium-high heat. Add the eggs in two batches and make two flat, thin omelets. Cool, roll up, and julienne.

5 Heat the shoyu and remaining 1 tablespoon sugar in a saucepan over medium-high heat. Add the lotus root and carrots and sauté until there is no more liquid in the pan, about 5 minutes.

6 When the rice is done, quickly empty it into a large bowl and remove the kombu. Add the vinegar mixture, folding it in until the rice cools. Add the julienned eggs and sautéed vegetables into the rice and mix. Press into a 9 × 13-inch (23 × 33 cm) baking dish. Sprinkle furikake on top.

7 Heat the remaining 1 tablespoon oil in a saucepan over medium-high heat. Add the mushrooms and onion and sauté until translucent, about 5 minutes.

8 In a medium bowl, combine the mushrooms, onion, crab, mayonnaise, and sour cream. Layer on top of the rice. Bake for 25 minutes, or until the top is golden brown. Let cool before cutting into small rectangles.

9 To serve cold, refrigerate overnight and cut before serving. Serve alongside cucumber sunomono and roasted nori or on its own.

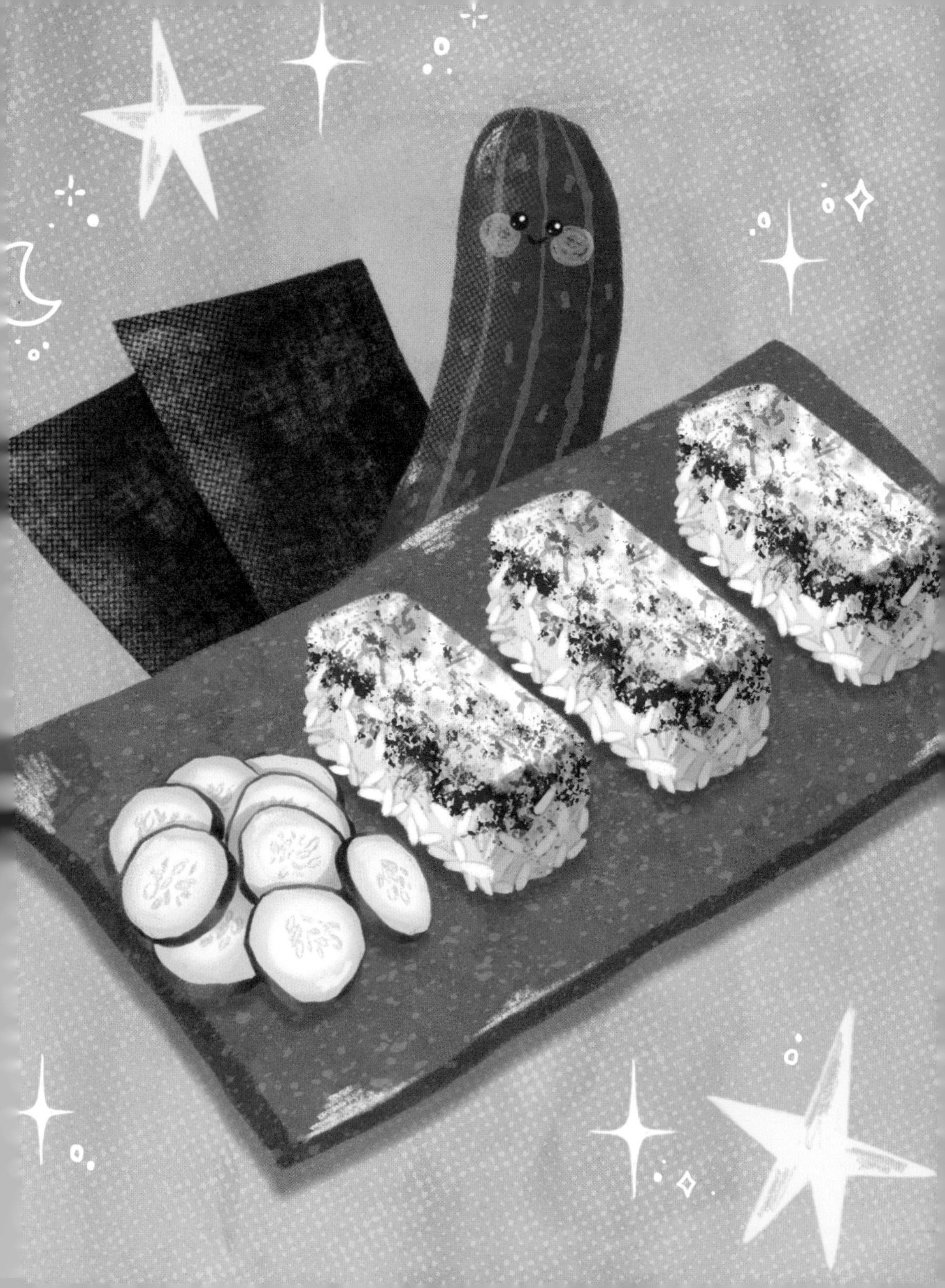

→ AUNTIE MARY JANE'S CAULIFLOWER NO TSUKEMONO (PICKLED VEGETABLES) ←

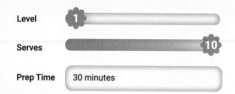

Level	1
Serves	10
Prep Time	30 minutes

My Auntie Mary Jane is a great cook, and her pickled vegetables make an ideal side dish for ramen—the tartness of the vinegar brine complements a rich ramen soup.

Ingredients

1 head cauliflower, broken into bite-size pieces

1 small onion (I prefer Vidalia), sliced

1 carrot, sliced

3 or 4 ribs celery, sliced

1 tsp red pepper flakes

Brine

1 cup (240 ml) white vinegar

1 cup (200 g) sugar

3 cups (720 g) water

4 tbsp kosher salt

1 Prepare an ice bath. Blanch the cauliflower, onion, and carrot in a pot of boiling water in separate batches for 30 seconds each. Return the water to a boil for each batch. Remove the vegetables and plunge into the prepared ice bath.

2 Heat the brine ingredients—the vinegar, sugar, water, and salt—in a medium pot over high heat. Bring to a boil for 3 minutes, or until the sugar dissolves, stirring frequently. Remove from the heat and let cool to room temperature.

3 Put all the vegetables in a container or glassware that can be covered. Pour the cooled brine mixture over the vegetables and refrigerate for at least 8 hours, or until ready to serve. They will keep for 1 week in an airtight container in the refrigerator.

⋧ KIM FAMILY POTATO SALAD ⋦

Level	1
Serves	8
Prep Time	35 minutes

My wonderful Korean friend, Soo, gave me this recipe. For this recipe, the order that you add your ingredients is important. The apples are added at the end, so they don't brown, and the Parmesan is added after the potatoes so that the cheese can melt into the mixture.

Ingredients

2 tsp salt, divided

3 medium russet potatoes, peeled and halved

3 eggs

3 slices pancetta, diced

½ cup (80 g) red onion, diced

½ cucumber (I prefer English cucumber), halved lengthwise, seeds removed, and thinly sliced

3 gherkins, halved lengthwise and thinly sliced

1 carrot, shredded

3 apples (I prefer Honeycrisp or Fuji, but any sweet variety works)

½ cup (40 g) shredded Parmesan cheese

¾ cup (175 g) mayonnaise

¼ cup (60 g) sweet pickle relish

3 tbsp mustard (I prefer grainy mustard)

½ tsp black pepper

1 Boil a large pot of water for the potatoes, then add about 1 teaspoon of the salt to the water. Add the potatoes and boil for about 25 minutes, or until a knife can cut through them easily.

2 Meanwhile, place the eggs into a separate pot of cold water, fully covering them. Bring to a boil. Once boiling, immediately remove the pot from the heat and cover. Let the eggs sit in the hot water for 10 minutes. Prepare an ice bath while waiting. After 10 minutes, place the eggs in the prepared ice bath for 3 minutes, then crack and peel them. Cut the eggs into bite-size pieces, yolks included. Add to a large bowl, big enough to mix all the ingredients without being crowded.

3 Add the pancetta, red onion, cucumber, gherkins, and carrot to the bowl.

4 Drain the potatoes and set aside to cool. When cool, cut them into bite-size pieces. Also cut the apples into bite-size pieces. Add the potatoes, apples, and Parmesan to the bowl with the other ingredients. Add the mayonnaise, relish, mustard, salt, and pepper and mix until well incorporated.

5 Refrigerate and serve cold. It will keep for 3 days.

→ MIKE'S ARARE (JAPANESE RICE CRACKER SNACK) ←

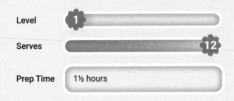

Level	1
Serves	12
Prep Time	1½ hours

This is a Japanese American rendition of *arare*—a rice-cracker snack seasoned with soy sauce. My brother's brother-in-law's, Mike, recipe is hands down the best. He was inspired by his wife, Mary, who wanted him to learn how to make it. It's everything you want in a snack: salty, sweet, and crispy. One handful and you're hooked.

Ingredients

1 cup or 2 sticks (225 g) butter

¾ cup (180 ml) corn syrup

2 tsp shoyu (soy sauce)

¾ cup (180 ml) vegetable oil

1 cup (200 g) baking sugar

2 boxes (each 12 oz, or 340 g) Rice Chex cereal

2 bottles (each 1.7 oz, or 50 g) furikake (available at most Asian markets or online)

1 Preheat the oven to 250°F (120°C).

2 In a medium saucepan over medium-high heat, combine the butter, corn syrup, shoyu, and oil until the butter is melted.

3 Lower the heat and whisk in the sugar until dissolved. It should be the color of butterscotch and have a creamy texture. You should have a total of 3 cups (720 ml).

4 Pour one box of cereal each into two large tin-foil pans or roasting pans. Add 1½ cups (360 ml) or half of the mixture over each pan of cereal, mixing well until the cereal is lightly coated. Pour 1 bottle of furikake over each pan. Mix well.

5 Bake for 1 hour, mixing and turning over cereal mixture every 15 minutes.

6 Let cool before serving so that the cereal can get crispy.

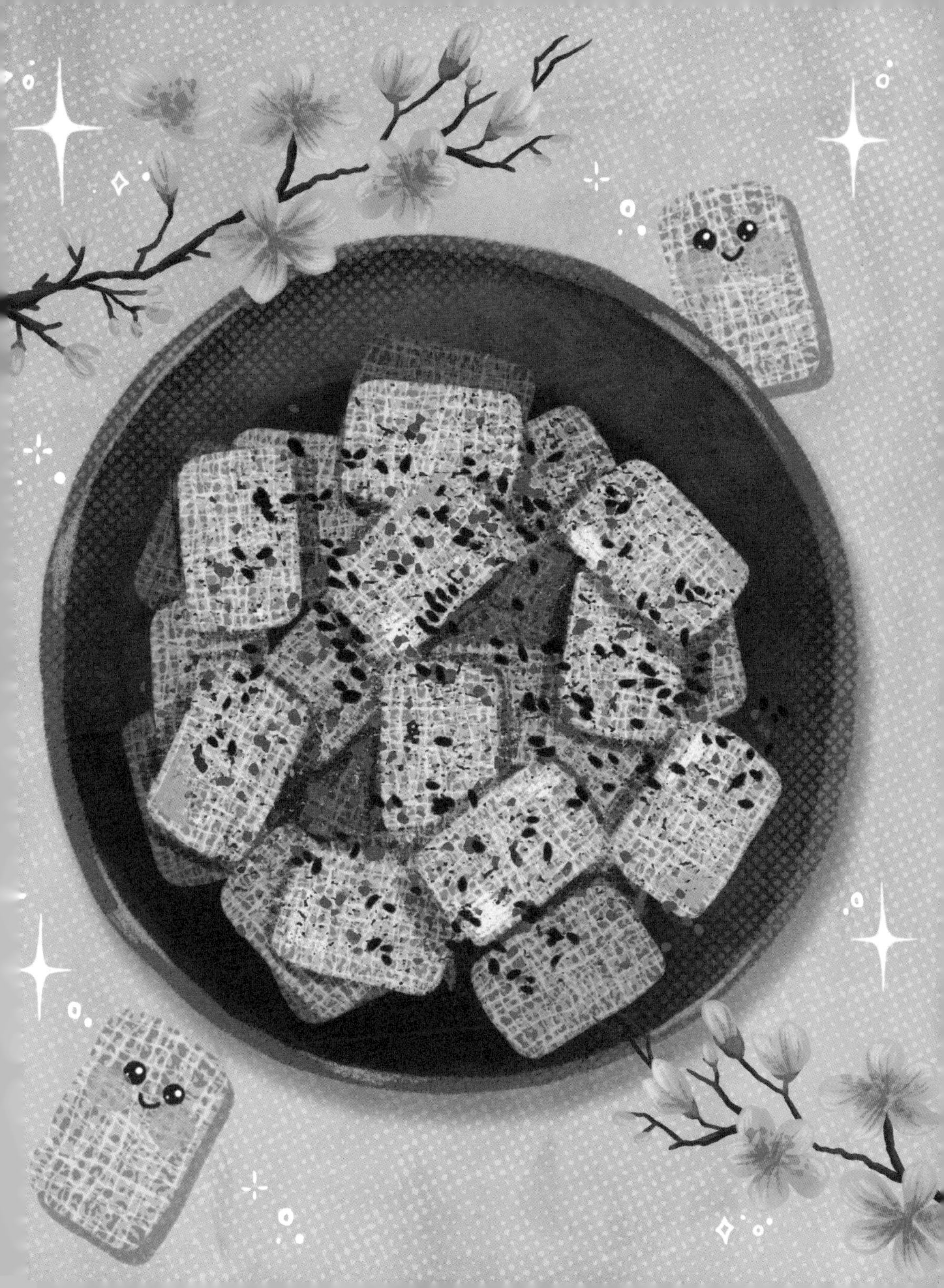

→ GYUNIKU KOROKKE (BEEF AND POTATO CROQUETTE) WITH KATSU SAUCE ←

Level	2
Makes	20
Prep Time	1 hour

I never refuse the offer of a *korokke*. It is one of my favorite Japanese comfort foods. I love the super-crisp coating and its smooth, fluffy potato filling. The katsu sauce that you dip it in provides the zing that brings it all together.

Korokke

1 tsp salt, plus more to taste

4 medium potatoes, peeled and quartered

2 tbsp olive oil

½ onion, diced

½ lb (225 g) ground beef

¼ cup (60 g) heavy whipping cream

2 tbsp sugar

2 tbsp shoyu (soy sauce)

Black pepper

4 eggs

2 tablespoons water

½ cup (55 g) flour (I prefer whole wheat flour)

4 cups (460 g) panko bread crumbs

Vegetable oil, for frying

Katsu Sauce*

¼ cup (60 g) ketchup (I prefer low-sodium)

1 tbsp shoyu (soy sauce)

1 tsp Worcestershire sauce

You can also substitute store-bought sauce.

1 To make the korokke: Boil a large pot of water with the 1 teaspoon salt. Add the potatoes and cook for about 30 minutes, or until a knife can cut through them easily.

2 In a large skillet, heat the olive oil over medium heat. Add the onion and cook until translucent. Add the beef and cook until no longer pink, making sure to break it up into very small pieces with a wooden spoon.

3 Drain the potatoes and use a potato ricer or masher to mash them in a large bowl. Add the beef-onion mixture, then add the whipping cream, sugar, shoyu, and a liberal sprinkling of salt and pepper. Combine well until the mixture is ready to form small patties.

4 To make the katsu sauce: Whisk together the ketchup, shoyu, and Worcestershire sauce in a small bowl until incorporated.

5 Beat the eggs with the water, then prepare a dipping station with the eggs, flour, and bread crumbs. Dip each croquette in egg, then flour, then egg again, then bread crumbs. At this point, you can freeze any croquettes you are not using in a freezer-safe container for up to 1 month.

6 Fill the same skillet used earlier with about about ½ inch (6 mm) or half the width of a croquette of vegetable oil and heat over medium-high heat. The oil is ready when a pinch of bread crumbs fries up quickly. Don't overcrowd the pan; fry 3 or 4 croquettes at a time until golden and crispy. Transfer to a wire rack, do not let them touch.

7 Serve warm and drizzle some katsu sauce over the top.

CRISPY TERIYAKI CHICKEN WINGS

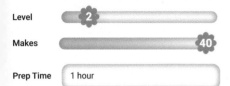

Level 2

Makes 40

Prep Time 1 hour

We make these once a year for New Year's, so it's a special treat for all of us, but they are also great as a side dish with ramen. Warning: they are extremely addictive!

Sauce

1 cup (200 g) sugar

1 cup (240 ml) shoyu (soy sauce)

2 tsp grated ginger

¼ cup (60 ml) mirin (sweet rice wine)

Chicken Wings

2 cups (480 ml) vegetable oil or enough to fill the saucepan about 1½ inches (4 cm)

1 cup (110 g) flour

1 cup (240 ml) water

3 ice cubes

2½ lbs (1.1 kg) chicken wings, washed and towel-dried

1 To make the sauce: Combine all the sauce ingredients in a small saucepan, bring to a boil, then lower to a simmer and leave it.

2 Meanwhile, make the chicken wings: Prepare a wire rack on an aluminum foil–lined cookie sheet.

3 Heat the oil in a medium, deep saucepan over medium-high heat.

4 Combine the flour and water to make the batter. Add the ice cubes to the batter to keep cold, continuing to mix as the ice melts.

5 The oil is ready when a very small amount of batter added to the hot oil fries up quickly.

6 Add the chicken wings to the batter in batches so that none are touching. Fry in batches until both sides are brown and crispy, turning with metal tongs halfway through cooking.

7 Dip the fried chicken wings in the simmering sauce for about 5 seconds before serving.

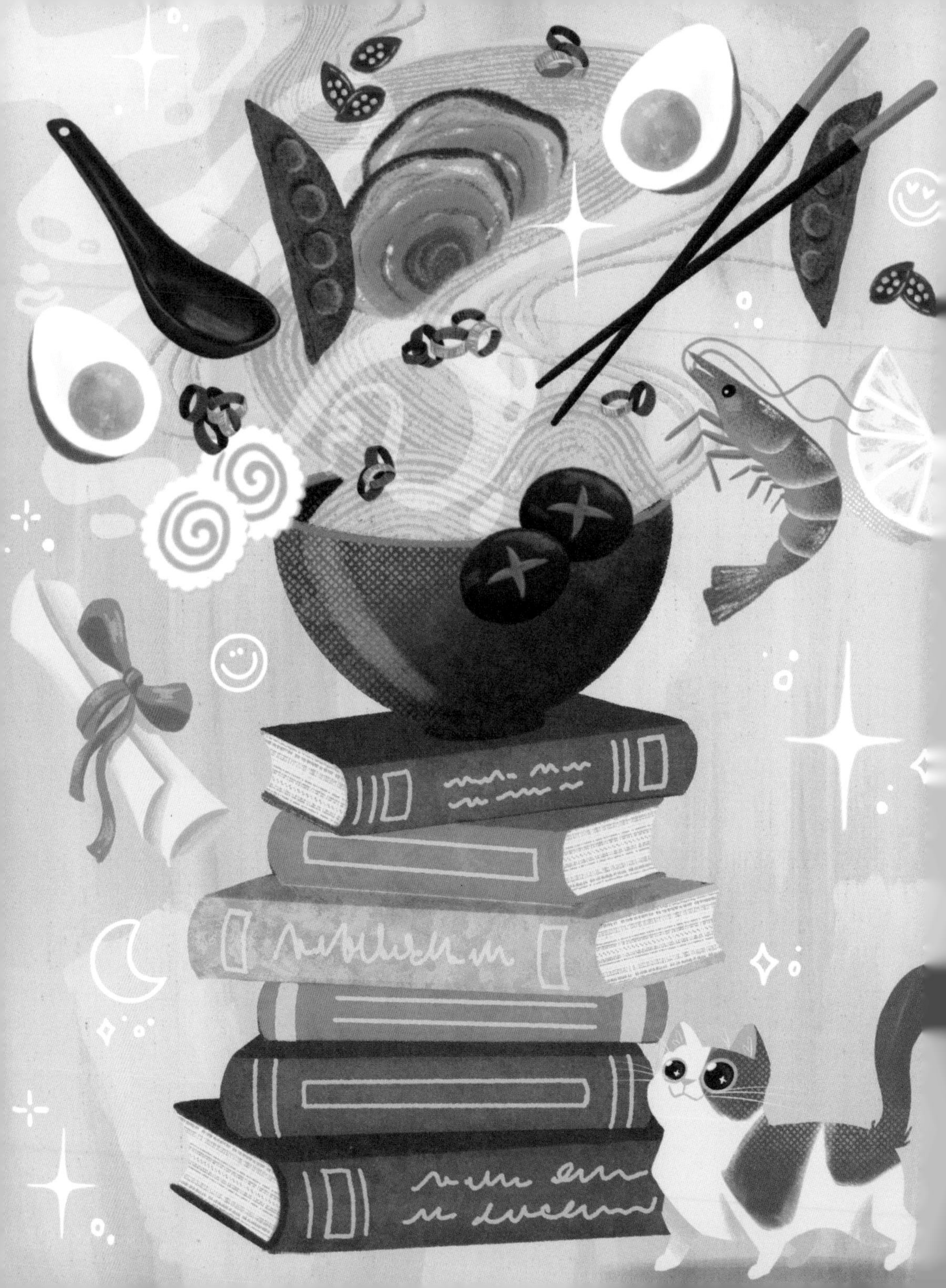

⇢ RAMEDUCATE YOURSELF ⇠

It wasn't very long ago that as far as most Americans were concerned, ramen was a block of dried noodles that was sold in a plastic package with a tiny envelope of mysterious seasonings, and it wasn't found much outside of college dorm rooms and the ateliers of starving artists. This "instant ramen" was developed by Momofuku Ando, a Chinese-Japanese businessman as a way to deal with post-World War II food shortages. It's only in the past decade that most Americans, including myself, have learned about the more traditional-style ramen made with long-simmered broths and artisan noodles that even appear on the menus of four-star restaurants.

My own ramen education took me from watching *Tampopo*, the classic movie about the Japanese love of food and search for the perfect noodle, directed by filmmaker Juzo Itami, to a more hands-on one in Japan. While there, I enrolled in an intensive ramen-cooking course and toured the ramen shops of Tokyo with one of the city's best-known ramen bloggers. Not only did I immerse myself in the culture of ramen, but I also learned a lot about myself as a Japanese American.

Sensei Rikisai at the Miyajima Ramen School in Osaka taught me that ramen was introduced to Japan at the end of the Edo period in the late nineteenth century when the country finally allowed visitors. Before that, the country had been formally closed to all foreigners. The Chinese came and introduced the noodle, lamien. The Japanese quickly changed the name to ramen and sold it as street food. Around this same time, the Portuguese brought over a wind instrument called a shawm. The Japanese adapted it into what they call a charumera, which was used by the ramen sellers to signal buyers to their carts. Ramen's popularity began.

I was lucky to have Brian MacDuckston, an American living in Tokyo who blogs about his favorite food at *Ramen Adventures*, as my guide to the ramen-yas of Tokyo. I asked him for a brief summary of the current state of ramen in Tokyo. Here's what he had to say:

When the dish that would come to be known as ramen made its way from China to Japan, it was quite simple: noodles with a firm bite and a light broth, really meant only to keep the noodles hot and add a bit of flavor. It was easy to prepare in large quantities, quick to cook the noodles, and was well suited to feeding many people in a short amount of time. Burgers and fried chicken may be commonplace in modern Japan, but in the past one hundred years, ramen was the ultimate fast food.

It wasn't long before moms were cooking ramen at home. With the advent of modern preservatives, the home-cooked ramen family meal could be as easy as a big pot of instant noodles, or as complex as handmade everything—soup from scratch topped with the family's secret-recipe chashu. Most home meals lay somewhere in the middle—fresh noodles from the local noodle shop, a light chicken stock kicked up with umami-rich ingredients, and some roasted meats sourced from a nearby butcher. This was dinner for many modern Japanese families, and the effect of the past few decades are being felt around the world today.

For many who grew up in Japan, ramen is deeply nostalgic. Slurping is probably the most fun way to consume food, and ramen doesn't just encourage slurping— it practically requires it. So with the current generation of adults longing for their favorite childhood food, ramen shops have had to take things further. Known in Japanese as kodawari, chefs are paying extreme consideration to details.

If slurping alone isn't nostalgic enough, local varieties of ramen do even more to instill a sense of hometown. Some, such as Hokkaido's famous miso ramen, use locally sourced ingredients, such as miso, corn, and rich butter, to recall the flavors of the far north. Other areas, such as Hakata with their thick pork tonkotsu ramen, are more about the style. Hakata is home to hundreds of late-night yatai, or street stalls, that sell stinky, porky, delicious ramen well into the night. Other styles, such as Kitakata ramen, seem to mirror the simple countryside life. Kitakata ramen is light enough to eat for breakfast, an activity enjoyed by many before heading off to work in the rice fields.

With the kodawari boom, many home cooks have been able to experiment with customizing their bowls. The Internet means that specialty ingredients are just a click away. It is these extras—high quality kodawari ingredients and local flair— that have elevated ramen from a simple noodle soup to the gourmet level that it stands at today.

As you explore the world of ramen, you'll see how this regionality plays in the different soup bases and styles. Sensei Rikisai taught me that ramen is made up of three building blocks: a stock that is the base for everything; a small amount of tare, or a highly packed flavoring base, that is added to the stock to determine what type of ramen it is; and a fat that makes everything milder and balances the flavors. Tare, when used as an adjective, becomes dare, as in shiodare, or strong salt flavor component. He described it as a perfectly staged play with each component having its own necessary role. With the exception of my Tonkotsu Base recipe (see page 16), which Sensei Rikisai taught me to make traditionally, I've simplified my other recipes and combined some of these building blocks to make it easier for the home cook.

The four main types of ramen that can be intermixed and changed by the stock, the tare, and type of fat added are Miso (miso paste blended in), Shio (a light salt component), Shoyu (mainly soy-sauce based), and Tonkotsu (creamy pork soup). The only thing that's a bit confusing is that Tonkotsu is a soup on its own, so you might see a Spicy Misodare Tonkotsu Soup, which is a combination of a Spicy Miso as the strong flavor component and Tonkotsu Soup. And a good soup has to have umami. My cooking course taught me that there are three kinds of umami: glutamic acid umami, which comes from ingredients such as seaweed and chicken; isocyanic acid umami, which comes from ingredients such as dried fish and mackerel; and guanylic acid umami, which comes from ingredients such as shiitake mushrooms and pork. Believe it or not, umami is very scientific—it's not just the fifth flavor sense that no one can describe. Aside from the umami factor, the texture of the noodles is vital to a good bowl of ramen.

Noodles can be made with varying levels of gluten. To understand this, for instance, a baguette has a medium-high level of gluten, whereas tempura, sweets, and cookies are low in gluten. Ramen noodles are in the semi-high gluten category. Most ramen chefs mix up the types of flours they use in their ramen noodles to experiment with these gluten levels. You can also vary the percentage of water mixed with "baked baking soda," or kansui powder (see page 25) to make a noodle that has a certain density. Noodles can be skinny, fat, flat, and so on.

What are the characteristics of a good bowl? The perfect density of soup brimming with depth and layered flavor; salt content that's not overpowering; handmade noodles that are firm yet springy and hold up to the soup; and fresh toppings that have been given as much attention as everything else.

INDEX

A

B

C

N

O

P

⋛ ACKNOWLEDGMENTS ⋜

One of the last emails I received from my husband, Dave, the week my cookbook was due, read: "I would be lying if I said I won't be happy when it's done!" Then he added, "Are we still having cheese ramen tonight?" and signed the note with a winking emoji. That pretty much sums up my life writing a cookbook.

My friends would say, "How do you do it all?" and the answer I would give them was "I don't. It's nuts." I gave up my marketing consulting business to devote myself to the cookbook and be at home for the kids. I found that when I took time out for myself, which I desperately needed on occasion, my family would get the short end of the stick because I'd have to make up the time working on recipes, instead of taking care of them. My daughter, Maggie, was initially excited to be my noodle maker but then she asked to be paid. I don't think my son, Ryan, washed his face the entire year because I was too busy to notice. And when asked at preschool to describe what I did, my daughter, Ellie, would say, "Sitting at the computer" and "Drinking juice (aka wine)." I gained ten pounds of ramen weight, but luckily, Dave told me he's never been into petite women. I turned "lunch with girlfriends" into "come over and try some of my ramen." So, we learned to adjust. I guess the answer to the question of how do I do it all is that I couldn't have done it without my village of friends who pitched in when I needed help and a super-supportive and forgiving family who always told me that the last ramen I served them was the best one they've had yet. Love you, guys, so much.

⇟ ABOUT THE AUTHOR ⇞

Amy Kimoto-Kahn is a yonsei, a fourth-generation Japanese American, and a mom of three who lives in Boulder, Colorado. She is a graduate of the Miyajima Ramen School in Osaka, Japan, and has taught a popular series of Asian-inspired cooking classes for Williams-Sonoma. She shares her Japanese American homestyle, kids-will-like-it-too recipes on her blog, *easypeasyjapanesey*. When she isn't cooking, she runs a mom-focused marketing firm, Fat Duck Consulting, that she founded in 2008. You can visit her website at www.easypeasyjapanesey.com.

This edition published in 2025 by Rock Point,
an imprint of The Quarto Group,
142 West 36th Street, 4th Floor,
New York, NY 10018, USA
(212) 779-4972
www.Quarto.com

First published in 2016 as *Simply Ramen* by Race Point Publishing, an imprint of The Quarto Group,
142 West 36th Street, 4th Floor, New York, NY 10018, USA.

Rock Point titles are also available at discount for retail, wholesale, promotional and bulk purchase.
For details, contact the Special Sales Manager by email at specialsales@quarto.com or by mail at
The Quarto Group, Attn: Special Sales Manager, 100 Cummings Center Suite, 265D, Beverly, MA 01915, USA.

10 9 8 7 6 5 4 3 2 1

ISBN: 978-1-57715-505-8

Digital edition published in 2025
eISBN: 978-0-7603-9437-3

Library of Congress Control Number: 2024943248

Publisher: Rage Kindelsperger
Creative Director: Laura Drew
Editorial Director: Erin Canning
Managing Editor: Cara Donaldson
Cover Design: Camila Gray
Interior Design: Evelin Kasikov
Illustrations: Camila Gray

Printed in China